MARGOT

Love in the Golden Years

Jottings between two lovers

2003 – 2019

Remembering Margot C.G. Thomson

31 January, 1938 – 16 January, 2019

Crescent Beach, Surrey, British Columbia

by

Ben Nuttall-Smith

Margot – Love In the Golden Years

Authors: Margot Thomson and Ben Nuttall-Smith

www.bennuttall-smith.ca

Publisher: Rutherford Press

www.rutherfordpress.ca

For information, contact:

Rutherford Press,

PO Box 648

Qualicum Beach, BC, V9K 1A0 Canada

info@rutherfordpress.ca

www.rutherfordpress.ca

Printed in the United States of America and Canada

ISBN (paperback)   # 978-1-988739-39-7

ISBN (ebook)   # 978-1-988739-40-3

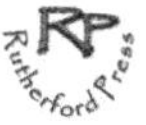

Greatest gift of all

Knowing you for all these years

Thank you for your love

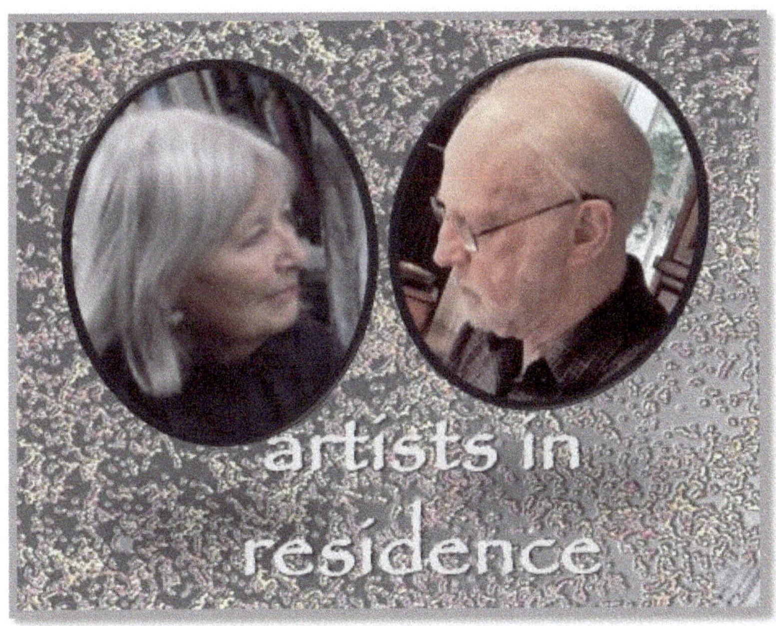

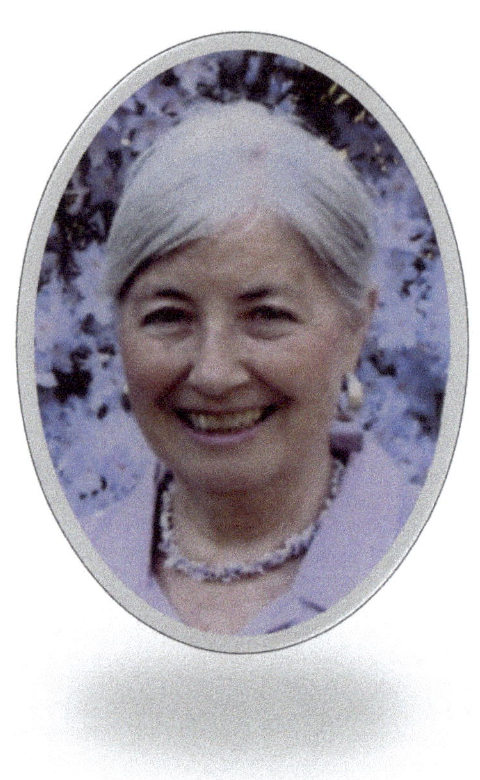

Margot Charlotte Gage Thomson

<u>31 January, 1938 – 16 January, 2019</u>

Margot was born in Regina, Saskatchewan,

attended Vic College 1955-57,

Graduated from U.B.C. Honours Psychology, 1960.

Margot's 25 year career as a psychologist,
initially in government services and later in
private practice, involved therapeutic work
with children, families and individuals.

Following her retirement, Margot designed
and painted on glass and became a prolific
painter on canvas. Much of her work can be seen at
http://www.margotthomson.ca

As reflected in her professional and personal life,
Margot's deep interest in and
love for people was paramount.
Margot has touched, inspired, encouraged,
loved and transformed so many.

Peace Arch News obituary

Margot

Forward

This collection is my attempt to honour the one person I have loved beyond all others for the past sixteen years. Margot not only encouraged my scribbles during those years, she influenced and encouraged others during that time as well as producing many gems of her own. Thus I include those of her works I have been able to salvage as well as snippets of correspondence between the two of us.

* * * * *

After a lifetime of being lost, I found in Margot the one person who would not only love me as I was, but would believe in me and my early attempts at writing. Here was an artist who fully supported both my poetry and my painting. With Margot as primary editor and coach, I soon learned to trust her judgement and make almost all suggested changes. For sixteen years under her influence, and touched by her love, I grew and thrived, producing and publishing a variety of books. In my painting, despite our totally different styles and techniques, Margot would suggest subtle touches of colour and shading that brought added dimension and perspective to mountains, trees and figures.

Margot offered encouragement and praise but was not afraid to admonish when needed. With Margot, I slowly learned to be in the now, and to accept people who thought and believed differently than I. She taught me to see other points-of-view and to treasure people as they are.

Her beliefs were quite different from my own, yet she supported mine to the point of accompanying me to church on numerous occasions. I had never before known someone who not only believed in me but taught me to believe in myself.

Margot was mentor, guide, lover and partner in all things.
I miss her dearly but, when I listen carefully, I still hear her
voice. She's with me still.

* * * * *

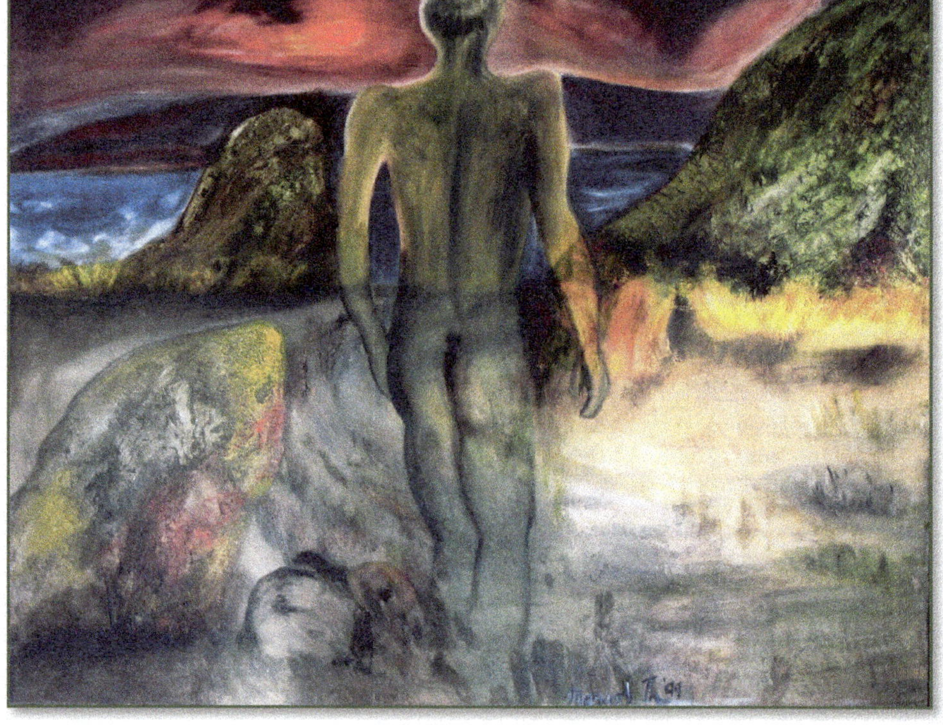

1 *Facing West*
1999 — 3' x 4' — oil on canvas

The secret to undying love

The secret of our love was always
100% both ways
Never "What will you do for me?"
Rather "What can I do for you?"

Don't ask. Just do.
I didn't fall in love with you –
I decided to love you.
That's a mystery I can't explain.

You saw me as I was
warts and all
And took me as I was
A battered soul.

Your heart, broken by betrayals,
remained loyal to one who needed you.
I respected that love until his passing
Accepting your pain.

Love is not a feeling
Love is a decision.
The opposite to love is not hate
But selfishness.

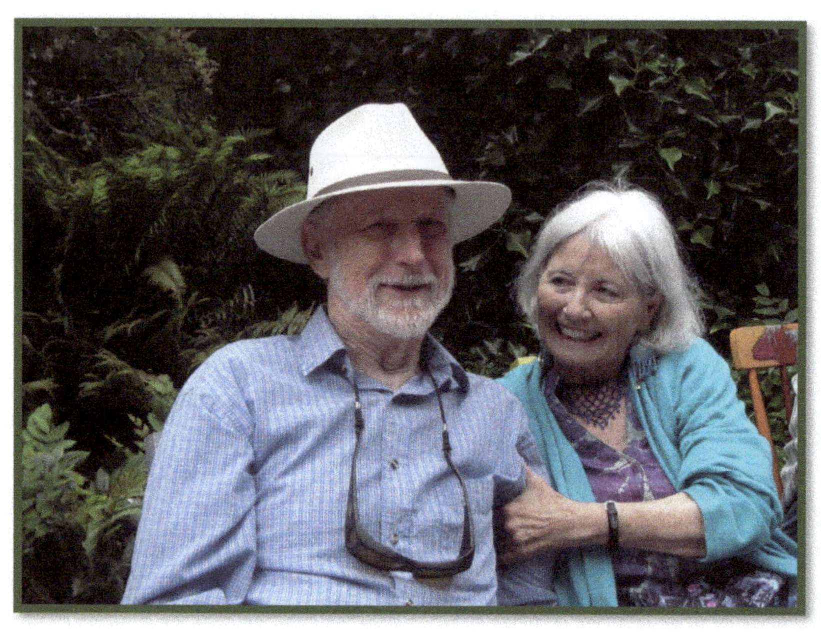

5

Celebrating:

Celebrating Water

Water is necessary for all of life.

We drink it when we're thirsty and we wash things in it.

We play and splash in it and we swim in it.

In boats we explore and fish on it.

Clouds block out the hot and drying sun, and can be so beautiful.

Rain cools things and makes trees and plants grow

Snow is fun to ski and sleigh on. And Ice! Fun to skate on!

From snow we make igloos, snowmen, and snowballs.

Snow is also beautiful – falling from the sky, coating everything in white

And snowflakes! What wonderful designs!

We love the sound of water babbling in brooks, lapping or pounding
against the shore, crashing from water falls, splashing from
fountains.

Water and the sun make rainbows. Full of colour!

Misty water makes mysterious fog.

Our favourite thing? A day at the beach by a river, a lake,
or the sea.

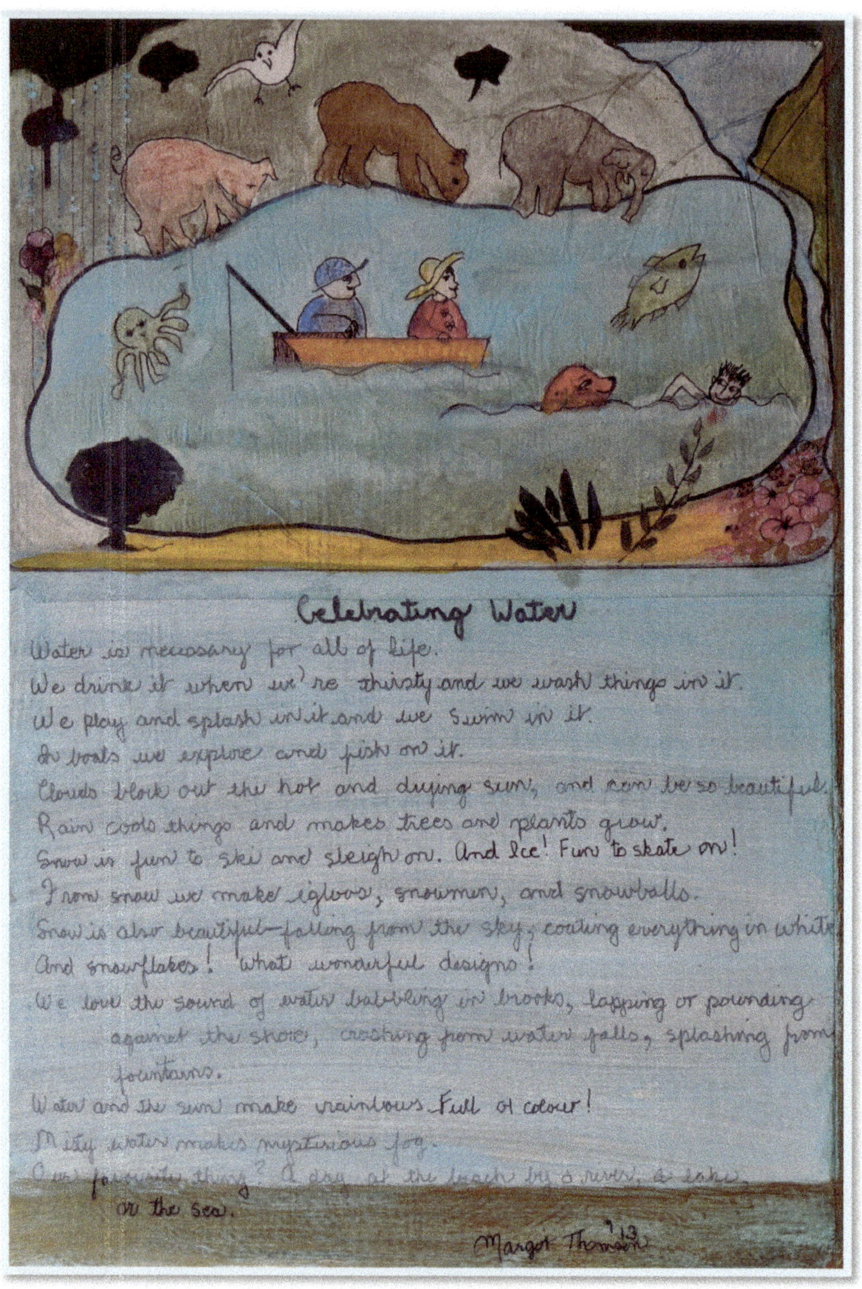

2 *Celebrating Water*

Celebrating Trees

Trees are beautiful

They are a home for birds in their nests, spiders in their webs,

and children in their forts.

They are a place for swings, a place to climb

Trees block the glare of the sun, and frame the stars and the moon.

They make great sounds — their leaves rattle in a light wind, their

limbs roar in a big storm.

Trees shade and cool all the creatures. Fallen leaves create rich soil.

Tree leaves carry the season's colours — light green in the spring, darker

green in the summer, yellow, orange, and red in the fall and some

carry snowy white on their many evergreen tresses in the winter.

Tree trunks nurse baby trees when they fall, and become lumber to build

houses, and pulp for paper.

Tree sap makes delicious syrup.

Tree roots hold the soil from slipping away in the rain.

Trees store carbon and give us oxygen.

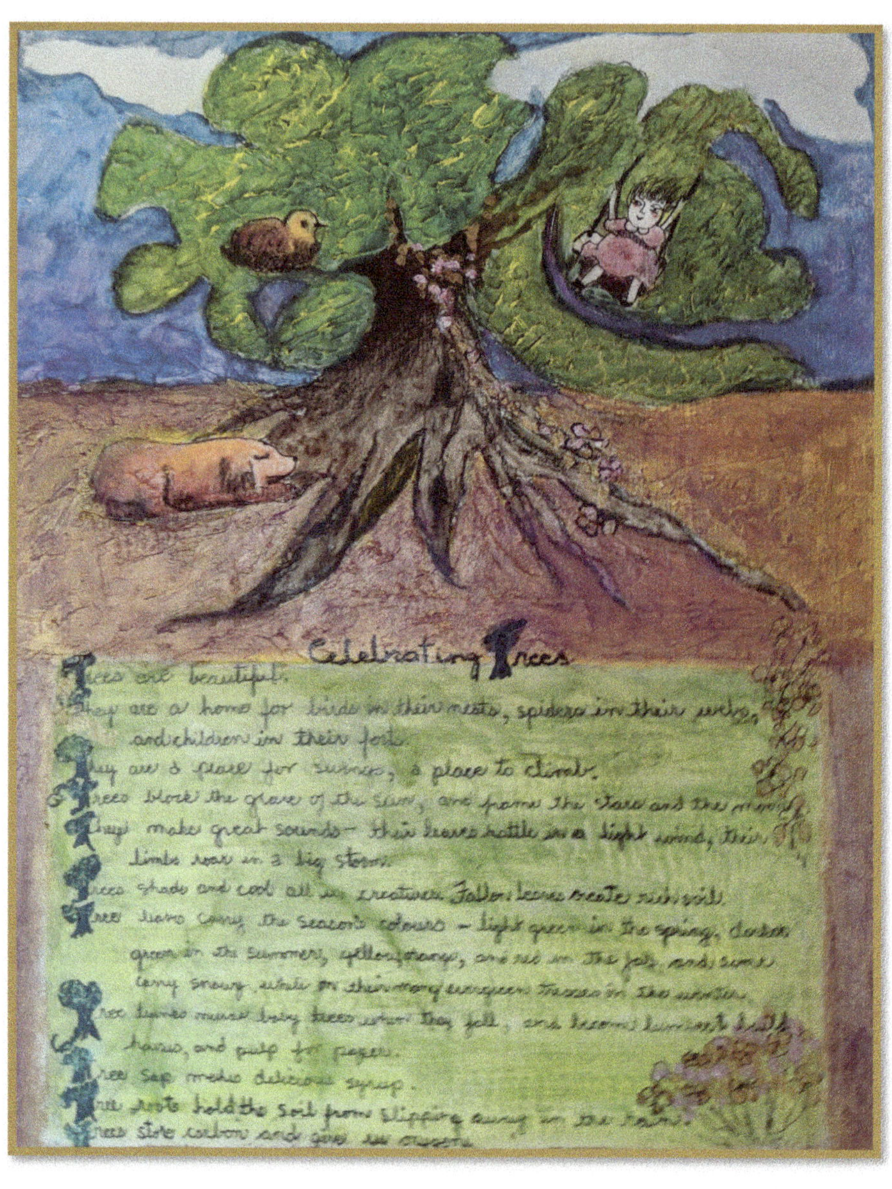

3 Celebrating Trees

Celebrating Children

Children are: spontaneous, innocent, enthusiastic,
curious, open, loving, capricious,
imaginative, mischievous, spirited,
affectionate.

Children enjoy: playing, jumping, running, yelling,
building, swinging, wrestling, dressing
up, singing, giggling swimming,
dreaming, showing off, hugging,
splashing, exploring, practicing, kissing.

Children love: toys, food, hide and seek, dolls, games,
animals, cars, water, picture books,
birthdays, parties, presents, surprises,
friends, candy, ice cream, mommies and
daddies.

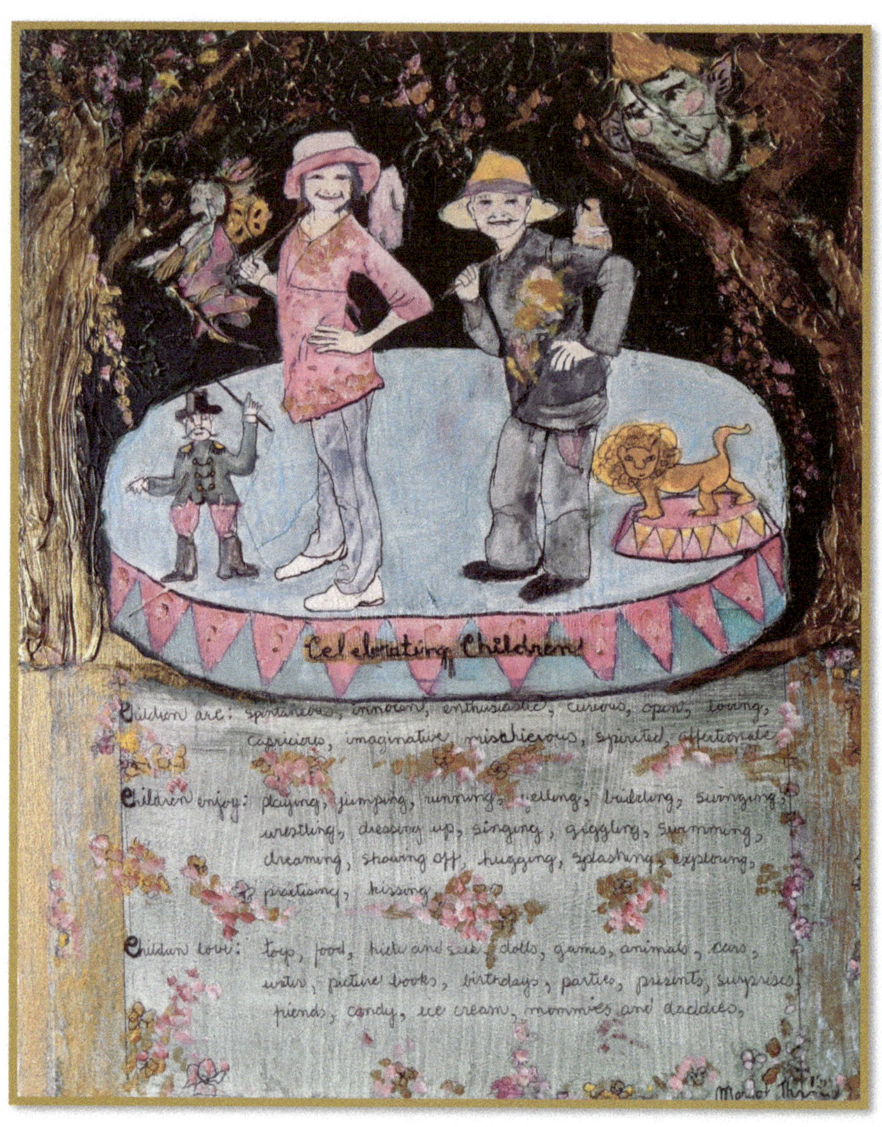

4 *Celebrating Children*

My Darling, my Sweet, my Charlotte, my Margot

Our recent discussions have given me added hope. And I've had three days to think about you and miss you and appreciate you all the more for the love and care and companionship you already give me. I am so fortunate to have you. I remember how lonely I was before you came into my life. I lived on resentments and persecutions. Now I live in happiness and hope for the future. You've put up with so much but, like a garden that needed a thorough weeding, look at how I'm blossoming in the warmth of your sunshine. You've renewed my own faith in myself and given me the capacity to be more for others.

I love the way my children and my grandchildren see you as part of our family – part of their families. I truly admire the way you are able to connect with Arianne and Xavier and with Heidi. And I eagerly anticipate your having the same connection with Cormac and Chris and Carol.

I look forward to the years to come and our growing love.

Happy Birthday my darling.

Ben   January 31, 2010

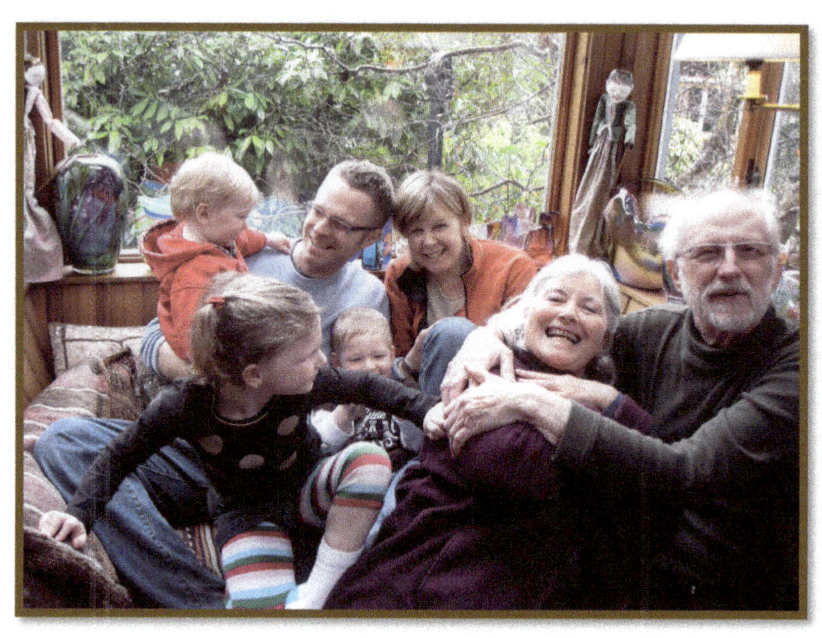

Roses for my sweet

Petals on your table top

Symbols of my love

My Darling, My Lovely,
My Sweet Ben----

You are such a Prize —

The best thing that could have happened to me at this time in my life.

Because of you I learn more, I accomplish more, I explore more, I feel more,

I have more fun, I experience more of my hidden mother feelings — which I had shelved until Arianne and Xavier came into my life.

You are so generous and patient with me and my friends. You give so easily of your time and your gifts and your intelligence and your knowledge.

And your sense of humour. And all the songs and poems you know. You are truly a treasure house of literary fun, beauty, and silliness. Good for me and others who are far too serious.

You are so supportive of us who are in need. Me about Taras. Alex about his illness, Heidi as a mother trying to find her happiness, Chris as a striving and independent father, husband, journalist, home builder, David as an unhappy person, all your writers who need support, your extended family – especially Louise, but all of the Papalardos, You are patient with my quirky friends – who shall remain nameless – just in case!

Thanks for all your help and patience vis a vis my crippled hand – and all the Christmas preparations.

You know I really can't think of a gift to give you – other than to tell my appreciation – that matches all the gifts you give me. You are an amazing man!

I love you

Margot Christmas, 2009

15

l have known love

Once I loved a pretty face

my heart beat faster than a speeding train

and took all breath away

with time and trial, love faded like a wilted rose

The train crashed

Our love has stood the test of time

padlock on the Pont des Arts

truer than all youth's passion

more beautiful with age

deepest caring; naught held back

shoulder message at the kitchen sink

morning touch — our eyes connect

so glad you're with me still

Happy Saint Valentine's Day my Darling

Ben   February 14, 2016

if

April 2003

silver hair

listen now

silver

not grey

but like

chinese silk

butterflies embroidered

if i were your hair

would you brush me?

earrings

white shell

glistening

listen

dangle, dangle

oh, to be

a white shell

earring

whispering in

your ear

grey sweater

warm

hugging your breasts

oh, to be a grey sweater

your grey sweater

i'd hug tight

and not stop

book on your lap

speaking to you

saying words

i dare not say

oh, to be your book

such things

could i tell you

if i were

your book

   if you blew a kiss my way

   i'd catch it

   and keep it in a jar

   and hold that jar to my breast

   and open the lid just so far

    if you blew a kiss

new poetry

you stepped into

my life

as new poetry

even to my jaded ears

as birds sing

spring songs

you smiled my way

and the sun escaped its clouds

you kissed my lips

with new life

you touched me

and i tingled

with poetry

Our Golden Years
My Darling

I was a shipwreck   foundering alone on a stormy sea

tempest tossed – swamped

You appeared – a lighthouse beam guiding me to saner shores

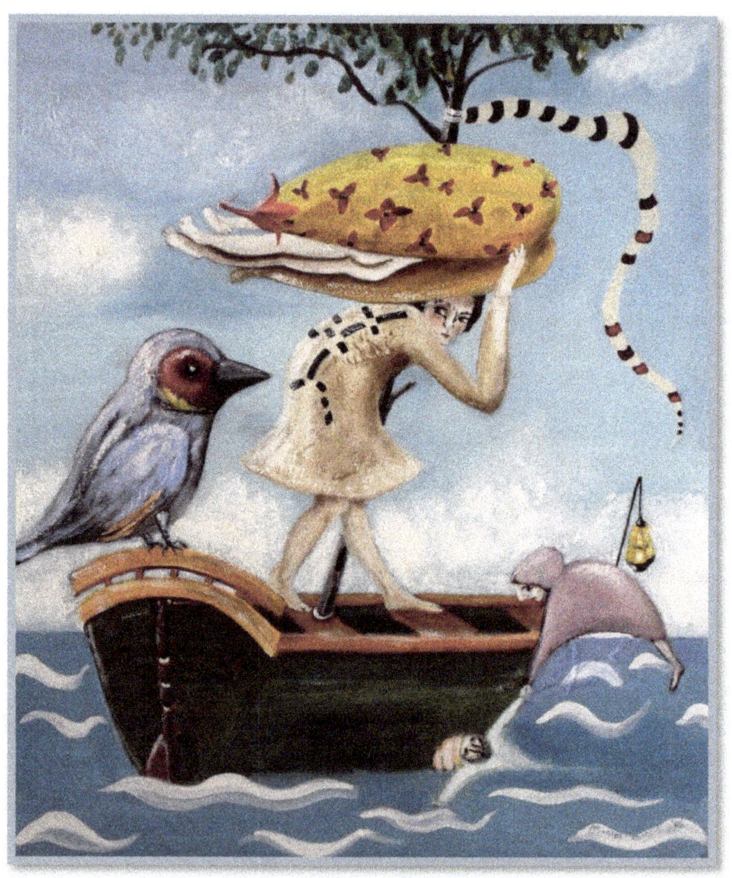

5 *Silently and Secretly*
2005 – 40" x 30" - oil on canvas

These years we've been together have brought my spirit to maturity.

Your love and gentle patience, soothed and helped heal

cancers of mind and heart.

My love, given without expectations, you returned manifold

I have loved you more than I have ever loved before.

We are frequently reminded one of us will move on

to the great unknown ahead of the other.

What that next existence will be, I cannot know.

Our lives, yours and mine, have earned happiness and peace.

I pray to be here for you, Throughout the coming years

to love you more and more as time goes by.

I'll be lonely without you. But I could be contented

in that solitude having known you.

I will love you forever.

Ben

BIOGRAPHY AND RELATIONSHIP TO MY WORK

Margot Thomson

I always put emotions at the centre of my paintings – my reactions to experiences in the present, informed by a rich and varied childhood lived in various family homes and boarding houses. I have carried these images and experiences into my work as an artist, psychologist/therapist, and activist.

I started life in a warm, extended family in Regina, Saskatchewan. I was born one year before World War Two. I remember every detail of living in my paternal grandparent's home in Regina – the water-pump at the kitchen sink, the smell of the big blocks of wash soap on the cellar stairs; the family as it gathered around the piano; watching the huge summer storms from the screened veranda.

I remember my maternal grandfather's CPR station in a small prairie town – the pail of cold drinking water, my

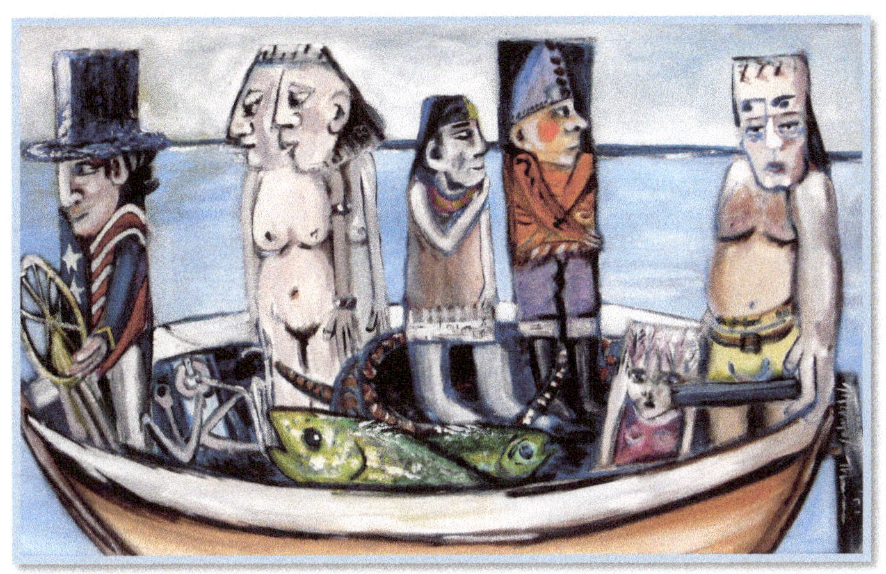

6 *In Thrall*
2001 – 30" x 40" – oil on canvas

grandfather's green eye shade and telegraph ticker, the steam-belching engines, and the mirages along the tracks that looked like the longed-for ponds; riding the garbage sleigh, with a bunch of kids, down the hill next to the station.

These early experiences, never forgotten fixed my attention to the surroundings and their meanings, and affected, I'm sure, all of my painting.

When I was five, my parents were separated, first by WWII when my father was wounded after landing on D-day, then by choice. All the six young men from both my families were in the war, and the family talk around the kitchen table was about their fears for their "boys" overseas. This affected me

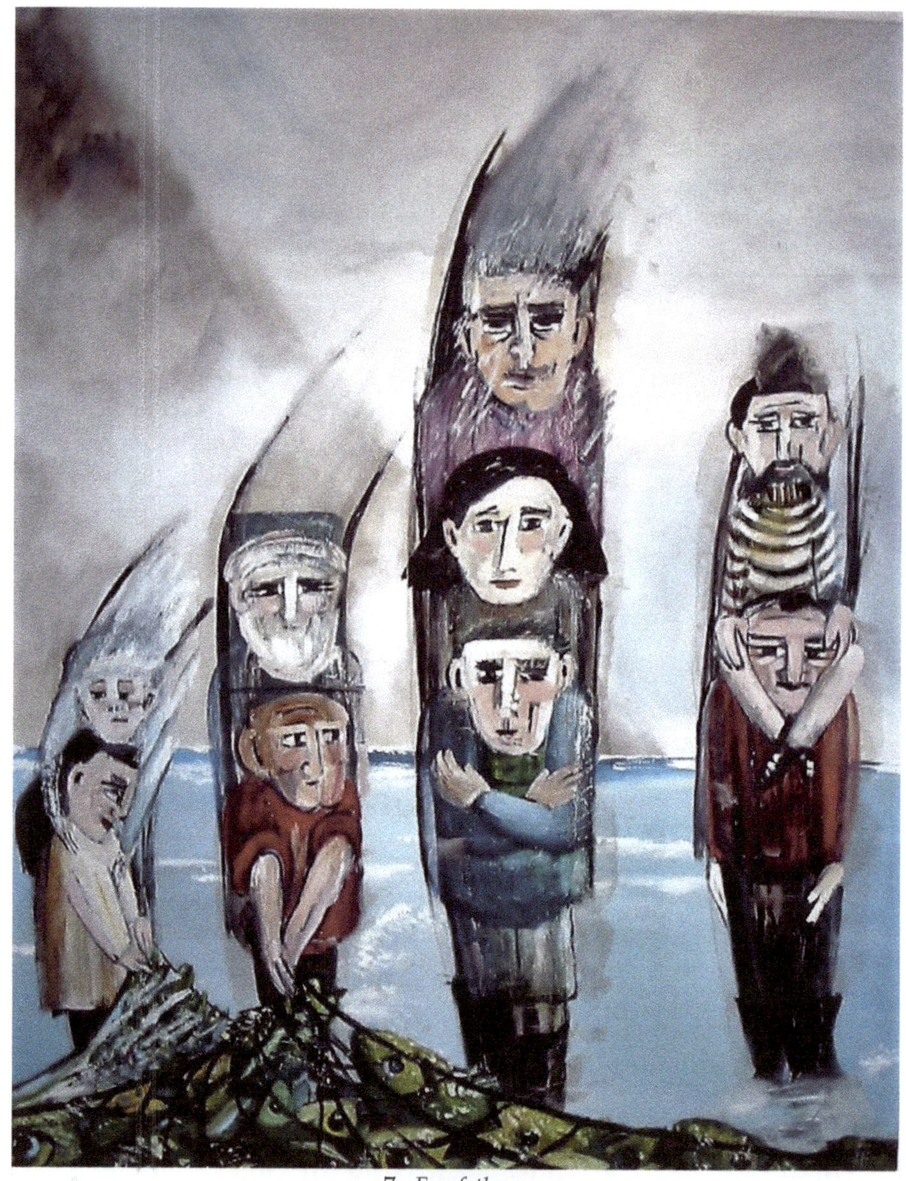

7 *Forefathers*
2002 — 4' x 3' — oil on canvas

Following my parents' separation, my mother and I moved to Victoria and boarded in a variety of homes with "outsiders", creating complex and wonderful memories, as well as the painful feelings of separation and loss. We lived with three spinster aunts who resided in a gorgeous Victorian-era house on Dallas Road by the sea. They wore long black gowns, long beads, and "cow-pies" piled on their heads. They knew Emily Carr, who had lived only blocks from them, and had stories about her. Living by the sea I experienced the storms, the fog, foghorns, the fabulous storm-formed trees, the sea smells, the beaches and the fields along the seafront. This continues to be a magical place for me and motivated THE DALLAS, and THE VESSEL AND THE SEA paintings.

Later, we lived with a Rumanian "Ma" and her "sister" (actually daughter), an English duchess who dressed in men's clothes, and an asthmatic seamstress who was later brutally murdered. The house was squeezed between a dairy and a Pentecostal church. My mother's and my room was lit by the lurid and warm neon lights of the car sales lot across the street.

I know my love of and interest in people and relationships comes from these early times and pervades my work. Also those night images and illusory, and complex identities — as well as the horror comic books my roommate cousin and I fought over with neighbourhood kids — probably informed the CARNIVAL paintings. I had a red dog then. He stars in the RED DOG paintings and has made appearances in other series.

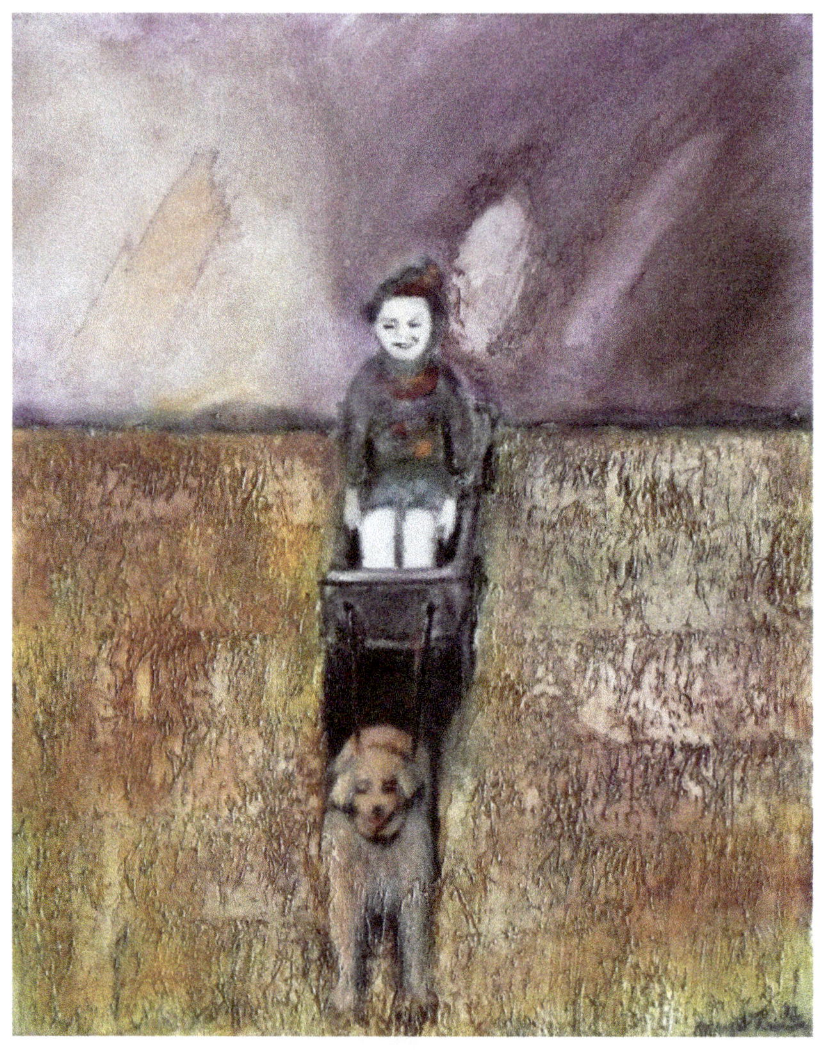

8 *The Dog Cart*

2015 – 20″ x 16″ – oil on canvas

My parents reunited in my teens, and those were happy times — but it is the earlier memories that created my tendency to timeless images, and informed my work as a therapist and activist. These very intact memories have created a lasting love and respect for the ambiance of past eras, a sympathy for the marvelous variations in how people get through life, and a deep interest in evoking, through my art, both the beauty and the horrors of life as it unfolds in the present.

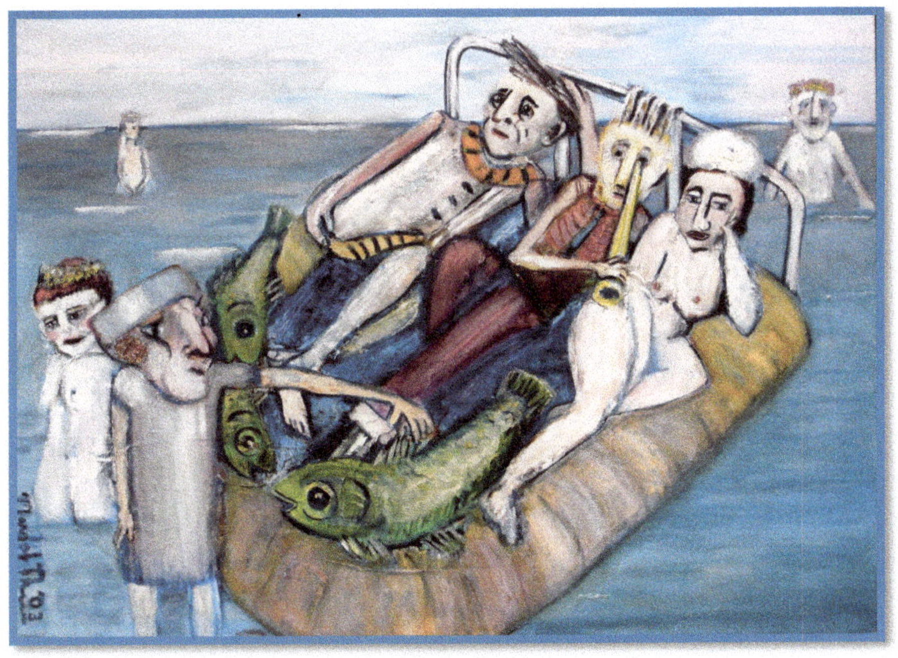

9 *The Uninvited*
2003 — 3' x 4' — oil on canvas

Glassworks

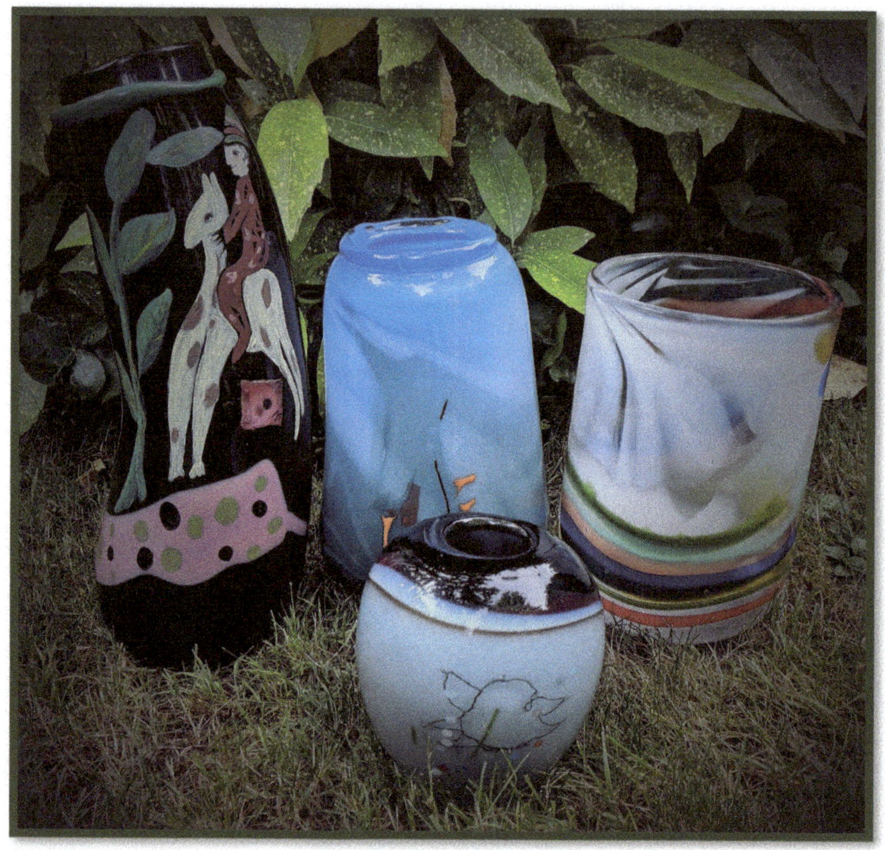

Margot's glassworks received international acclaim.

Her pieces are found in the Corning Museum of Glass, Corning, N.Y., U.S.A.;

Minister of Foreign Relations, Simon A. Consalvi, Venezuela;

Department of External Affairs – Ottawa;

Vancouver City.

AWARDS FOR GLASSWORK:

1992   Simon Fraser University Gallery Burnaby, BC - Award of Merit - Juried

1991   Langley Centennial Museum, Langley, BC - Individual Juror's Choice

1990   Art Association of BC - Bank of Hong Kong Atrium - Recognition Award - Vancouver. BC

1985   Crafts Association of BC - Maria Greczmiel Award

Margot's work was the feature article in *Glass Art Magazine* (U.S.) - 1987 Nov/Dec.

It was appreciatively covered in:

2003   Galleries West - Summer

1991   Canada Council and Ontario Crafts Council Catalogue, "Canadian Glassworks"

1991   Canadian Clay and Glass Museum, Boehmers Photo Calendar

1988   Peace Arch News - October

1988   Ontario Craft Council - FOCUS lll

1986   Arts Vancouver - Cover Photo - Fall

1985   Western Living Magazine - "Glass Acts" July

1985   Vancouver Sun, 27 July. "A Touch of Craft" - Section B , front page with photo.

         Edmonton Journal. 13 August. "Lively Arts"

1983   Edmonton Sun. 5 August, p. 55 - "Mute Art at the Muttart"

3/5/18 – ODE TO MY WEE HOUSEY

Margot – In contemplating leaving her

What I love – In the winter, sunlight dancing off the leaves of trees that poke their faces into our windows.

The dappling shadows of leaves papering our walls. The roar of the tall cedars bracing themselves against strong sea-winds.

The winter bird feeders attracting – first the chattering chickadees – then all manner of birds – Wilson's Warblers, smart crows who manage to force the feeders to fall so they can get "more". (In fact two crows, being all cuddly together managed to mate while I watched. I found myself saying "now they have something to "crow about!") Black squirrels come too.

Spring

The shy glances of bunny rabbits nibbling our grass as birds flit by – racing for a favourite tree limb – or chasing newly emerged bugs. In the summer, the racoon kittens tripping across the lawn with their mommy close behind. They eat our grapes with little hands – luxuriously – as though safe, sound and fulfilled.

I love thee dear housey with your apron of trees and bushes and grass. The dark leaves of the of the ivy falling carelessly from the trees. The cedar bean pole fence that surrounds and helps to privatize our garden – with the assistance of ivy.

I know the ivy is pernicious and will cause the ensuing owners pure hell – but more power to it, says I!

The brilliant colours of flowers in pots, Ben's marvelously surprising and beautiful blooming English garden.

The fort – so beloved by so many kids –Arianne and Xavier. Alannah and friends Baco, Lyman, Melissa, Carlene. And next to the fort - the hammock. You could swing and look up to the lofty cedar trees and ascend into oblivion.

The gazebo – pronounced "gaze beau" – so hospitable for sitting and reading, or for intimate conversations with best and beloved friends.

The short path to the sea, sand and mountains – so beloved by me. The sea, sand dunes, sky, clouds – ever-changingly delicious. To sit on the beach and see the melding of sea and sky into infinity creates unbearable longing in me – as does the lapping of the sea to the shore. Reading and drawing - inspired by these sights, sounds and smells is my very favourite pastime – I become so in touch with myself.

Walking out on the tide flats, shoes on, through beautiful tide pools full of life hiding beneath eel grass, clear water magnifying shells and creatures, worm sand pyramids – all the mysteries and memories of my childhood times on similar quests in Victoria.

Like me, my house is sick and sad that she contains me in her sick arms. I long to rescue us both. I know she knows that I'm leaving her to an unknown fate. Maybe to a death as she is ripped apart — my love of almost 50 years.

After all — she incorporated so much of my life — my mother's once hated fancy pink "French Provincial" chairs with their gracefully turned legs and back graced with carved wood flowers — all tufted and feminine.

My dad's light pink and slippery silken chair with comfy down-filled seat pillow — which was all covered with a (pink) curtain to prevent printers ink from Dad's ubiquitous newspapers soiling the delicate covering.

Mama's (she wanted me to call her this — with accent on the second syllable — exposing both her pretentiousness, and her wonderful sense of humour) collection of interesting things from Italy, Spain, and Chinatown, Victoria.

My collection of camel bags, rugs, and baggy pants from Afghanistan (imported by Carnaby Street Store, Victoria — in the 70's, of course). In fact, I still have my great collection of baggy pants from that era.

The dining table I stripped to a fine polish, and the spooled dining chairs that reminded me of Spain. My collection of chairs, tables, cabinets all from junk stores and all belovedly served me.

My wonderful studio — its' high skylighted ceilings battle the winter grey and enfold me in my creative moods and humour my messiness, and my need to be surrounded by little things that have become treasures — including memories of my glass paintings days. There's the chair that was once (again) my mother's exquisitely covered in a chinoiserie pattern — now covered — like an old lady in practical and fraying green — with ottoman. My Nanny's kitchen cupboard (one like it) carries all of my paints and things. An old kitchen table holds other helpful objects. And I look out on all the beautiful trees and houses of our neighbours.

I love being in here.

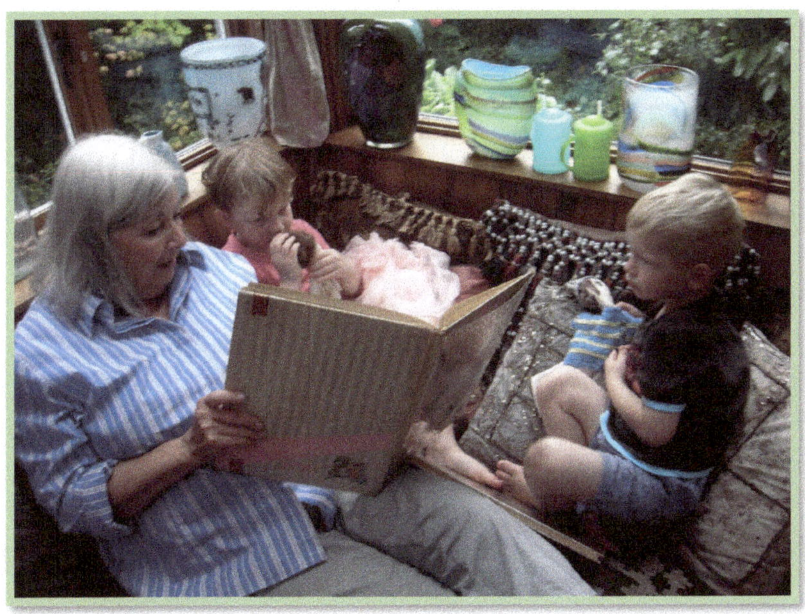

Elder Love

chips in the porcelain
treasured more now
than when we were new

beauty radiates without pretense

brittle handles
squeaky hinges
cracked window panes

eyes transmit unfeigned love

we shout not in anger
to ears slow in response
cobwebbed detours

bestowed without seeking

buildings somewhat tired
not ripe for demolition
candles still flicker

kisses sweeter than youth's passion

warm hearth
smoke in the chimney
hallways echo joy

intimacy beyond dreams

we approach the door
knowing one must pass through
empathy for one remaining

forever true

love is stronger
than all our years
strengthened with age

Greetings from Margot and Ben

As we age into our 80's, Ben and I are encountering some "blessings". They remind us that, despite working to stay healthy, and trying to keep up with painting, writing, and music, our bodies are sagging, begging for naps, and protesting with pain if we insist on doing what we've always done.

We haven't travelled like we used to – only a short stay in Puerto Vallarta last year. Even for a bit of entertainment - and to avoid unbelievable traffic jams and huge parking fees - we take fewer trips into Vancouver. With some trepidation, we've booked a winter trip to Cuba, and we might take a spring trip to England. We'll visit Ben's sister and cousins in Oxford, then on to the Cotswolds, and Cornwall.

We are mainly in good spirits. Ben's grandchildren give us much joy. And I think we laugh more than we ever have – sharing our memory problems and same old jokes, and same old stories, our trivial and funny misunderstandings (because of hearing loss), frustrations, and loss of body bits, and organ failures - with our equally dismayed friends.

So there you have it! We're learning that we can't "have it our way" much anymore! And yet life can still be a lot of fun!

Sending you love, and sympathy (just in case you know what I'm talking about!)

Margot

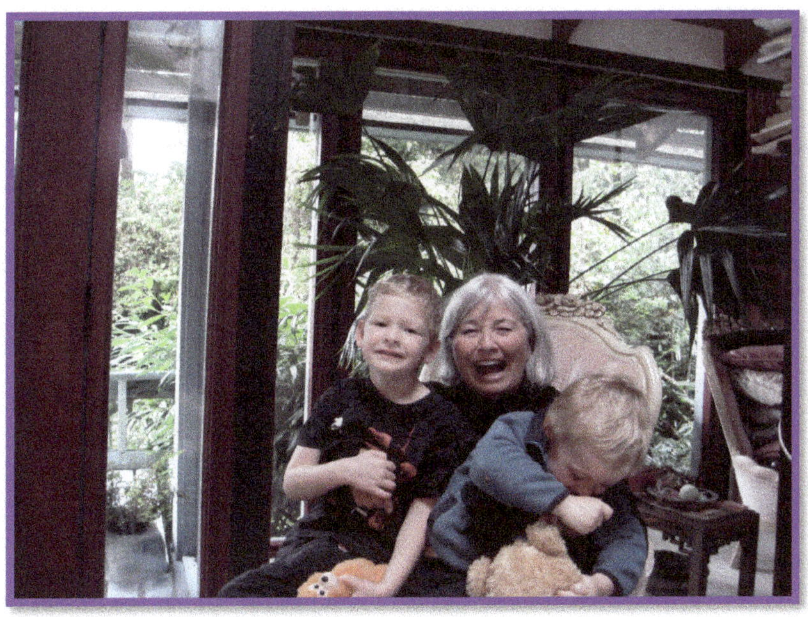

My Darling

*I count many blessings since kind fate brought us together
just short of fourteen years ago.*

*I almost frightened you away that spring evening following
your opening at Kurbatoff Gallery.*

*Your patience, perseverance, love and understanding kept us
together.*

You nurtured my spirit

saved me from my demons.

I bask in your affection and care.

I, in return, can only offer my undying love.

*   *   *   *   *

There's a corner lot in Crescent Beach

where wild birds come

to feed through winter's coldest winds.

Is it the fat you hang beneath the bower

or strains of music sweet that bring them by?

Perhaps they come to see the art

that hangs from every wall

reflected through warm windows.

Black-capped Chickadees

will sing your praise throughout the year.

"fee-bee, fee-bee, hey, sweetie."

I hear them now and thank you for their song.

January 31, 2017

You are all I want

Everything I'll ever need

Yours until the end

My Darling Margot

Thank you for the countless beautiful days and warm nights.

Thank you for so much love and tender caring.

Thank you for all that you give to our grandchildren, Arianne and Xavier

and to Heidi and Raul.

Thank you for loving Chris, Carol, and Cormac although, because of distance, we see far less often than we'd care to.

Thank you for being who you are.

Happy Birthday my darling.

Here's to many more happy travels together.

Ben   January 31, 2012

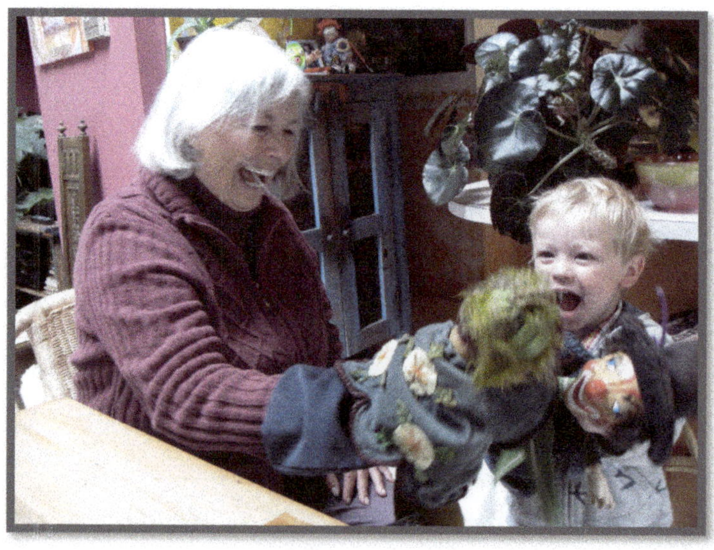

The Artist I Know

Were I to paint a picture to remind me of you,

I'd paint rose-cheeked faces,

Green fish and chickens on their heads.

Shading would be wind-blown trees

Along broad banks of ocean bluff

Where shaggy brown dogs lie down

By park-benched men,

Content in glorious sunny parks.

On the water, I'd paint boys standing in boats,

Every one of their faces having a story to tell.

I'd paint clowns and children,

Top hats, turbans, piggyback people,

Horses, beaches, happy times,

Even 'mongst tombstones

And tales of biblical proportion –

Your life's remembrances.

Most of all, I'd paint a happy artist,

An artist filled with love.

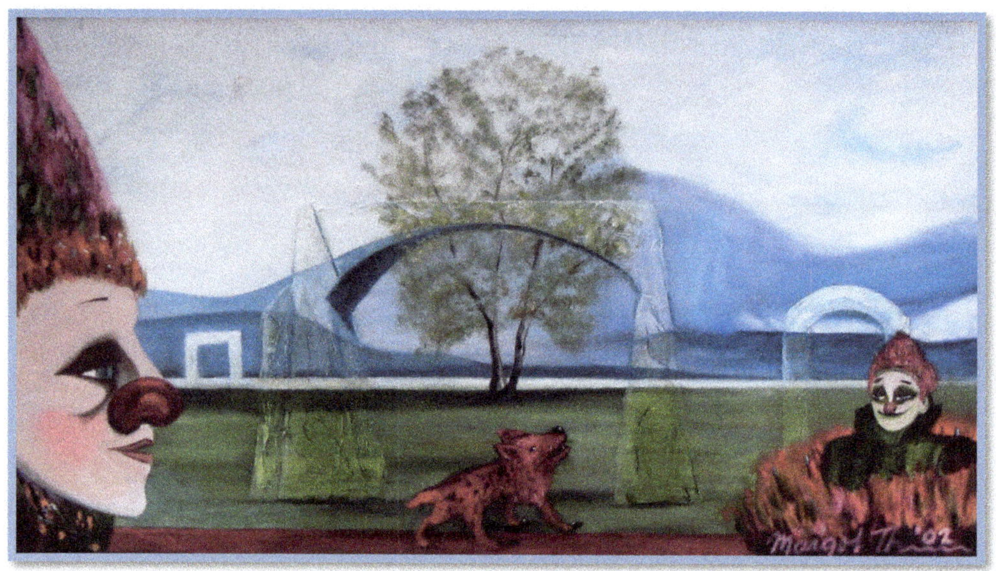

10 *Vancouver Phantasmagorique*
2003 – 30″ x 48″ – oil on canvas

She's All These Things –
and More

She's an artist, a lover, deep and sincere.

A brilliant, beautiful soul.

She listens with empathy.

No need for words;

You'll always know she understands.

She can think like a child

And sees into the mind and heart of a child.

She knows not only how to talk to children,

Level, eye to eye,

She hears what they're not saying.

Children are drawn to her.

Her home is filled with treats –

not candy – no bribery –

but toys: miniature dolls and bunnies and bears,

books and tiny houses with secret locks.

She has dress-up clothes and silk scarves

That float dreamily from upstairs landings

To Persian music and Stravinsky

Or Peter and the Wolf.

She laughs at delights in children's eyes.

She helps create stories and can appreciate silly songs,

Even knock-knock jokes and ridiculous noises.

An entomologist on the beach, she points out the tiniest creature.

She discovers the shapes of mythical monsters

In driftwood, seaweed, or rain-filled clouds.

She shares my tears when we watch sad movies,

When part of my childhood comes unraveled in a scene.

She reaches out to hug the wounded boy.

She's mine and I miss her when I'm away,

Especially in the rain.

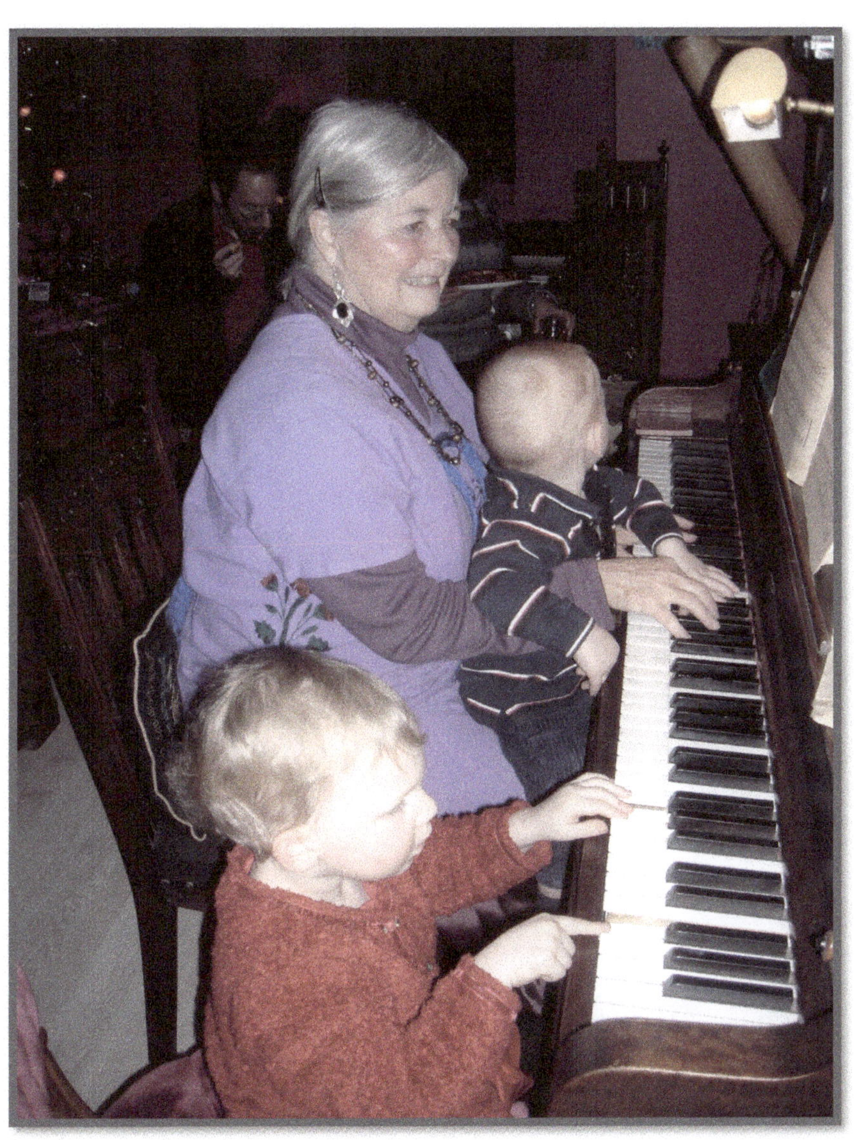

Why do I love you

Easter 2008

You asked me why I love you,

not if, nor how, nor when.

I'll attempt romantic turns of phrase,

or scribbles from "les écrivains d'amour"

in languages from all around the globe:

"Ich liebe dich", "Te amo", "Je t'adore",

I'll quote from Barrett Browning,

from Tennison and Crane,

from Burns, and Ford, and Blake to tell you how.

I'll spin you silken negligées,

cast roses at your feet,

and sprinkle you with fairy dust. Here's why:

I love you for sharing your home,

your friends and those you love.

I love you for your music and your art.

I love you for your hopes and for your dreams.

I love you for loving my family,

for taking my loved ones as your own:

my children, grandchildren, sisters, and their kin.

No one has ever been as warm as you.

I love you for your laughter,

I love you for your fears.

I love you for your empathy and tears.

I love you in the morning and in the evening.

I love you in the sunshine,

I love you in the rain.

I love you forever

no matter where.

You asked me why I love you.

My list runs for all time.

I love the way you love me,

the way you take my hand,

I love the way we dance together,

and the way you give yourself.

I love your gentle touch, your calming smile.

Most of all, my darling:

I love you because you're you.

REMEMBERING

Remembering my Aunt Elaine

Aunt Elaine was the youngest of five in the family of Glad and Ida Thomson. Glad, who had been a deputy minister in the Saskatchewan government lost his position when the government changed – and this was on the heels of the depression. So a few years before World War Two the whole family of young adults was pretty much centred at 2312 Cameron Street in Regina, the capital of Saskatchewan, each member having to contribute to the family coffers.

We had very hot summers with dramatic rainstorms, and extremely cold winters – but we spent a lot of time outside – in the summer at Wascana Lake – water skiing, and swimming, and in the winter at outdoor skating rinks or skiing behind cars. Elaine had two brothers, Ken, and Allan, and two sisters – Dorothy and Marion and they all had many friends who shared good times together. There was a lot of laughter, and Elaine I remember in particular because her laugh was a warm, throaty one – very contagious. Her smile was enormously radiant. And I loved her – she was fun.

She and Uncle Gerry met before the war and married in Victoria, where Gerry was stationed.

Elaine spent the war years surrounded by her family and friends – sharing letters from each of the boys who were overseas. Elaine's husband, brothers Ken and Allan, and brother-in-law Jack Bagnall, all served. Gerry served as a communications officer on the Prince David – which saw danger delivering our men to Juno Beach, Normandy, on D-Day. Her brother Ken, my father, who landed In Normandy on D-Day, was wounded in France on August 13. Her other brother, Allan, who was also serving in France, was able to meet Ken in the field before Ken was wounded. And brother-in-law Jack was taken prisoner by the Germans.

These were terrifying times for Elaine and her family – but letters my mother wrote to my father Ken were full of the camaraderie of the women. They would get together several times a week and go over the news – good and bad, find distraction by playing bridge, or going to movies. This created a greater closeness between my mother, Rhoda, Ken's wife, and Elaine. I was a named after Elaine – I was given her second name Marguerite.

My mother loved Elaine's freshness and vivaciousness – and I remember her as very light-hearted, warm and sympathetic. Nevertheless, she was constant in her desire to put a brave front on any suffering – one had to read between the lines to know her sadness. This was a Thomson trait – one must keep a good face on things.

In subsequent years, Elaine and Gerry would come up to Victoria to be with Gerry's family, and with my parents and me. We would vacation together up-island at Parksville or

Qualicum. It was a gay time – laughter and memories flowing, again a glow of ease and well-being emanating from Elaine.

She was known for her generosity of spirit and her great sense of fun and is remembered with much love.

Whispers in the night

Love you more than life itself

I will hold you close

Remembering my mother

RHODA MAY THOMSON

8 February 1914 – 31 March 2006

Rhoda was born in Harrowby, Manitoba. Her mother, Gage Allingham, was of Irish descent, and her father, Charles Whall, of Welsh descent. After struggling with the uncertainty of farming (which he had idealized – coming from huge, urban London) Charles happily moved to a secure position as the station agent for CPR in Kilalley, Saskatchewan during the depression years.

There were 5 children in the first family, Rhoda being the youngest. They lost their mother when Rhoda was only 3. Charles remarried and had 2 more children by his second wife, Alice. As a teenager, Rhoda lived with relatives in Texas and proudly sported her Texan drawl when she returned to Canada in her late teens. She met and married Ken Thomson when they both worked in the income tax department. I was born in 1938. Sometime later Ken "joined up" and was wounded two months after landing on D-Day.

Eventually the family moved to Victoria — which they considered Paradise on Earth — and congratulated themselves everyday on the lovely springs and lack of snow — and beautiful beaches and views of the mountains. Rhoda and Ken were very visually oriented and they made sure to live as close to views of mountains and sea as possible. Rhoda enjoyed, very much, the staff that worked with her in her position as head stenographer in the Registrar's Office in the Department of Education, and Ken loved travelling around Vancouver Island as an assessor for the tax department. He eventually joined the Provincial Succession Duties Department, and Rhoda followed her heart by obtaining teacher training, and teaching grade three at St. Margaret's school, truly loving every day she spent with the children — whom she found utterly delightful.

Rhoda was an avid reader, loved to play chess and scrabble with her friend, Marion Fraser, belonged to the same bridge foursome for years, worked for, and became president of the Victoria Symphony Society, and volunteered as a docent in the First Nations section of the Provincial Museum. She had an abiding love of animals and acted as a sitter for her daughter's and sister's dogs and cats. She and Ken enjoyed very much the social events afforded by Ken's association with the Canadian Scottish. They travelled in Europe and made many visits to Hawaii where Rhoda indulged her passion for studying other cultures - not being a beach and swimming person – as Ken was.

Their favourite times were their visits with me in Crescent Beach, where they enjoyed warm and fun-loving times. They both had beautiful voices and loved to sing together around her piano. Rhoda was a very bright person, an exceptional raconteur, who had gentle, loving ways as well as great wit and charm. She had a strong moral compass which, with her compassion for others, always helped her to a deep understanding for many points of view.

Her secret passion was writing murder mysteries – inspired by watching, for example, the Alfred Hitchcock series on TV. Another secret amusement was watching Groucho Marx – whose wry sense of humour matched her own. She also went "ga-ga" (her words) over the "big cats" – especially lions and tigers – that might appear on animal programs. Toward the end of her life, sadly, she developed dementia – staying sweet and loving to the end.

puddles

splish splash

white boots in the rain you beside me

your hand on my shoulder you look down

as I look up

now

I kiss your tiny hands memories of childhood you are gone

yet

forever here.

you threw candies to the children fed me hot rum and lemon,

better cure than mustard plaster

I slept in your arms.

oh, how I've loved you

love you still.

(written for Margot's mom's memorial)

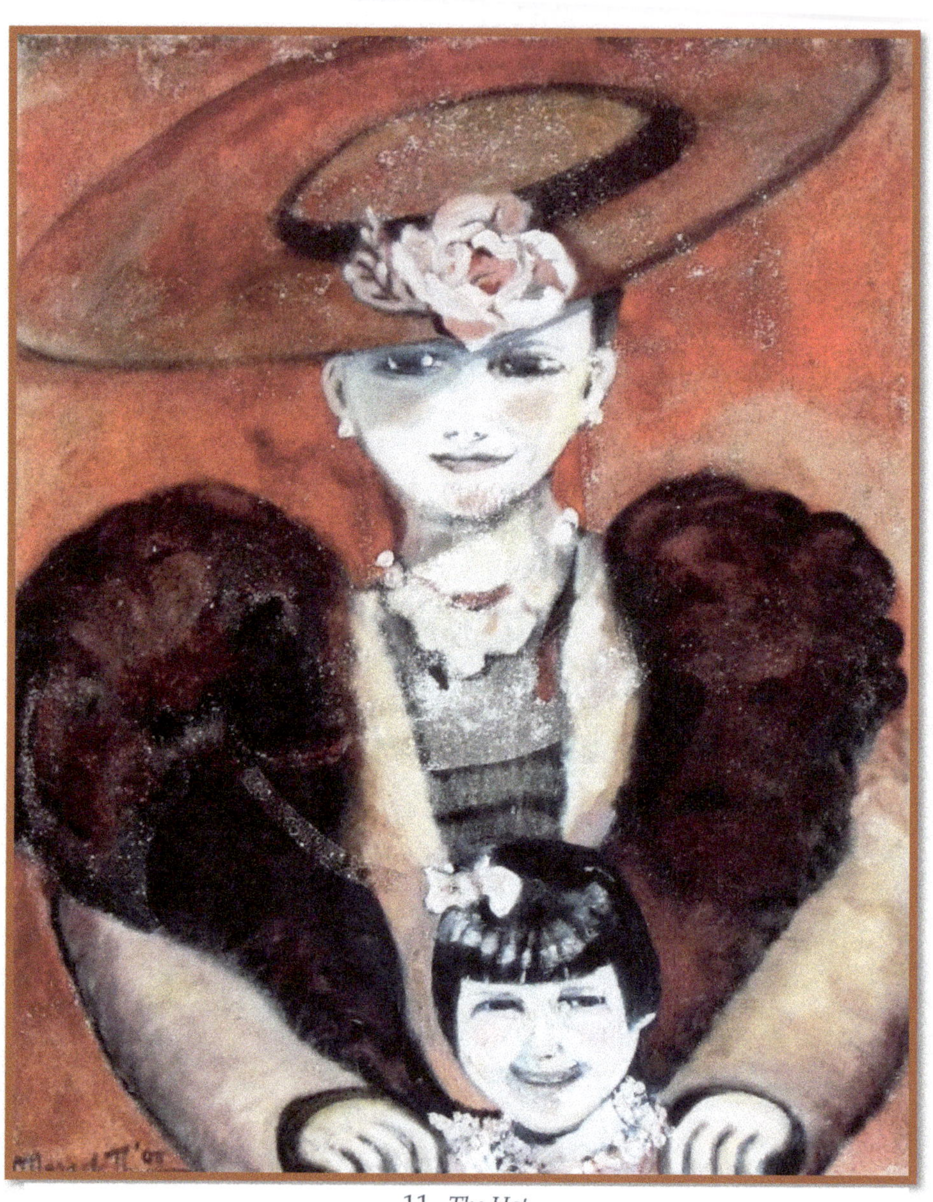

11   *The Hat*
2000 – 28"x 22" – oil on canvas

In memory of my mother

Rhoda May Thomson

8th February, 1914 — 31 March, 2006

THANKS to you all for your love and support - through all these years. And thanks to you who knew and loved and appreciated my mother.

Thanks so much to Diane and Sandy — who looked after mom while I was away — I knew she was in warm and gentle hands.

Thanks especially to my dear friend Ruth — who cared for my mother over the years, and enjoyed and delighted in her particular graces. Ruth, I'm sure, saved my mother's life recently when I was away being with Taras during his passing. It was really one of those moments when she could have passed away, but with Ruth giving her lots of love and attention, she waited until I got home, and then, I think decided to spend a little more time with me on this pale.

And Ben has been an angel to me. He was with me when I went to find that she had passed away moments before I got there — and he's been by my side ever since — holding my hand through all the arrangements and business that has to be done; also preparing the memorial piece for today – a huge job, and for the Times/Colonist in Victoria. He wrote the poem you'll see in the memorial – using words he heard me use as I was talking to Ruth about the pictures in the photo album. Doing all the work of cancelling our trip (which was to happen the next day) and reservations to Turkey and England. And he has comforted me in my moments of deep sorrow. I am so grateful and I feel so lucky to have him here at my side.

I'm going to tell you little vignettes about my mom which I didn't include in the printout that Ben and I prepared for family and friends who couldn't be here.

What a loss!

My mother lost her mother when she was 3 – so I think she knew how important it was to be there for me as I grew up. I remember all the little toys she made me from cardboard boxes – a stove, a fridge, little beds and chesterfields from scraps of material, and little boxes – chests of drawers from match boxes, a doll house with walls made from books, treasure chests, a rag doll whose face was coloured with Pancake Makeup. She encouraged my imagination and play, even in my teen years, "Don't burn your candle at both ends," she'd say; or, "Friday night is your night to howl." She never criticized my friends, not even one or two of my boyfriends who were a little weird. She loved my friends, in fact. I never felt pressure to perform at school. But I did feel some pressure when she let me know, somehow, that I might become a concert pianist.

Though she and my father separated for 6 years, she never bad-mouthed him — supporting my love for him.

My mother could "lose it" sometimes, but she always apologized, and asked me to forgive. In later years, if we were having a spat, she would do a hiss, like a cat and that would break the ice, and bring the laughter. We could go into giggling fits together over nothing.

She was very loyal to friends and family. I never heard her say nasty things about anyone, and she wouldn't let me. She always wanted me to understand the other person — which I couldn't always do as a child. She wanted me to be brave like my father/soldier — which meant I wasn't to cry — so I had to learn to cry as an adult. She was taught by her father to have compassion for others. For example, there were a lot of Germans in Kilalley, where Mom grew up, and during the war they would speak to my mother about their shame about Germany fighting us in the war — and she could do nothing but sympathize with their shame.

She was taught, and taught me, "To thine own self be true." She had a strong moral compass and, with her love of people, showed real compassion for the underdog or people from other cultures. She wept for our houseman, Wong, who sent back his earnings to his wife and children in China. She was very generous, in fact always made me wonderful lunches, and bought me beautiful clothes (she loved to dress well herself). But her generosity was for everyone. She loved animals. She rode horses as often as she could, even after we arrived in Victoria and she was a thrifty single parent. When we were away, she babysat my dogs and my aunt's cats, as a live-in sitter.

She was a private person, in a way — not given to sharing her troubles with the world. Probably because when she was a single mom and we were living with family or in boarding houses, that was a way to keep her dignity. In later years I started calling her Lady Rhoda because that perfectly reflected the persona she projected to the world — her daintiness, her love of dressing well, the place she wanted to be in the world. While we lived in apartments, when she and Dad got back together (she so desired a house) she wanted to project "well-to-do" — so she insisted, against my horror, that I be a debutant. I understand now — she was not secure in the established world of Victoria. These were minor little things about my mother's insecurities which I finally understood in my mature years. Yet she never complained. Never! She'd get mad, but would not complain. Her father gave her a real sense of her rights as a person and as a woman. I remember her talking to me about never being in servitude to anyone – which, because she was a secretary, initially (later a teacher), meant a lot to her. For instance, nurses were equal to doctors – that sort of attitude, which served me well when I found myself in the hierarchal mental health systems where doctors were at the top. It also got me in trouble because I wouldn't take guff from anyone.

My mother had her secrets. She secretly wrote murder mysteries, in a most baroque style, I have to say – naming people as Charles Dickens did, according to their role or personality in her stories. She had a dry, sometimes dark sense of humour. She loved to watch Groucho Marx.

She would go absolutely "ga ga" (as she would say) over the appearance of lions or tigers on nature TV. The Great Cats, she would call them.

She was a wonderful raconteur, and appreciated others who were. She loved men – some of us here have seen her flirt – but as far as I know she was never in trouble over it. But she sure found it difficult that my dad – a knock-out handsome, charming, gentleman guy – was a admired by women other than herself.

My parents had a super relationship in their mid years. My father absolutely adored my mother – admired her mind, and was a real gentleman with her. It was my mother who could swear like a trooper (within limits) when they had a "dust up" (mom's term). It was usually my mother who had to apologize for "losing it". My mother knew she had a real gem in my father and wouldn't push her luck too far.

I love to think of the love and respect they showed each other and me in everyday life. I loved the way she always welcomed me and my friends and partners with open arms. Whatever misgivings they might have had, they kept them to themselves — although it must have given them a lot of worry and pain to witness the sturm and drang of my life. I always knew they were there for me. I loved being at home with them on warm and cozy evenings. They are beautiful memories. They both had lovely voices and it was a real joy to play piano for them. My mother could recite lots from Shakespeare and other poets — something neither my dad nor I could ever do — so we admired her.

Mother worked for years as secretary to the Registrar in the Department of Education, and her boss, who thought she was too good for the job, encouraged her to go to University — which she did. She took education and happily landed a job teaching grade three at Saint Margaret's school. She adored the children, loved teaching and was very happy. This was during the years after I left home.

It was very sad for me to see my parents fade into dementia – you have all been around during these times so you know what I'm talking about. I had a great need to protect them from any hurt or indignity although I found Ocean View was ahead of its time in offering "gentle care" – a term used to connote respect for the person's needs, and their way of expressing these needs. I was fortunate that they spent the first 3 years after their diagnosis in a retirement home – which allowed them safety and dignity. My father passed away quickly – 6 weeks after being placed in nursing home here – but my mother has had 11 years in nursing care. I learned a different kind of love – perhaps what people have for their children – because of my mother's helplessness. I also learned that she knew my love because she stayed alive for me for so long.

She would have loved to be here – with us – chatting, laughing, loving, singing, being together. She loved us, loved being with us.

I will miss her – so will you who knew her.

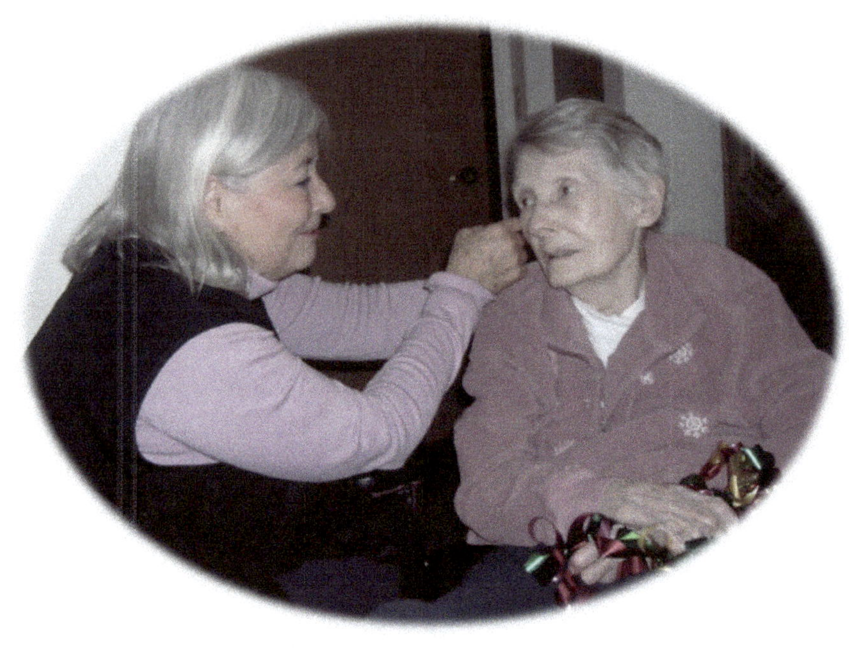

If I were a king

You'd still be my only love

Princess of my dreams

Alex

Alex, a young poet, was Margot's godson whom I also had the privilege of encouraging in his writing as well as teaching him a few tunes on the harmonica especially during his several hospitalizations. I must say, Alex also influenced me by his selfless caring for others, especially those who inhabited and gave light to his Street World.

Sadly, the young poet was driven by what one psychiatrist labelled "the most virulent schizophrenia he had ever seen", to end his life, leaving many to mourn his passing.

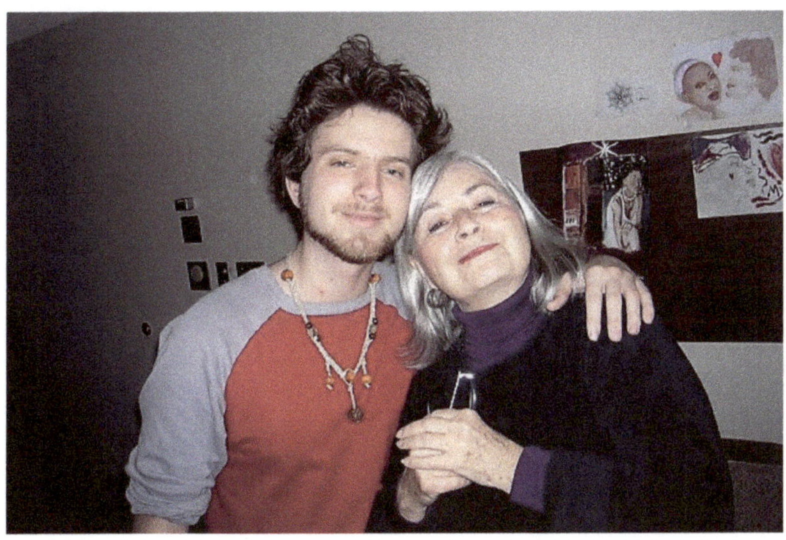

My Godmother's Blossoming House

Her lively music reaches rafters with flowering arms

as the rain patters.

She plays, the center of a colour tornado,

surrounded by paintings of naked ladies

dancing the tango.

A twinkly in her honey-coloured eye,

there's an invisible tiara

she earned on her many travels,

and the few lovers she's held close.

As she plays she flows, swaying with the music that

passes through her.

When she speaks she is articulate, low, raspy, artistic.

Her many notes enter my heart,

like rain magically trickling through the ceiling,

cleansing.

written by Alex

Xavier and Arianne

"I am the fastest man in the world!"

He shouts as if contending with hundreds of invisible opponents.

We wrestle in the grass and I cannot help but laugh at this smallness, as green fringes the eyes with moss.

We summersault in summer clothes, imitating the wind as it tumbles over our shoulders.

I love him too much for time; I have only known him a few hours, this animal of light.

There must still be a youngness in me, a green shoot that grows right up my spine.

I laugh so hard my soul begins to pour into my empty lungs.

This tiny Neanderthal shouts orders at a friendly giant:

"You are the Praying Mantis and I'm the Kung Fu Panda, and you gotta lose this time K? Cuz I am, I'm king, and I'm king of the world, K?"

Ah the injustice! To be beaten by this pitiful being, while in my greatness I have shattered the paranoid mirror.

Years of that stiffness lumping in the back of my brain crack and loosen. So many words, so many goddamned thoughts hunker inside me, a long shadow cast by the sun. A huge desert reaches its lonely claws into me. I fall into clear water; this garden, oasis of time. My desert dunes turn to waves, the cacti to mermaids, and the earthy trolls throw storms of boulders down the snow-capped mountains, and the arid desert loneliness transform into embraces from two ever so tiny beings.

Margot calls us into dinner.

They want to light the candles, and extinguish the candles. They want to know what every unfamiliar word means. They want to sit beside me. They reeeally want to sit beside me. And they do.

"Are you a man?" His 7-year-old sister leans over and asks, refusing to be shushed. "I am." "Ah, so young for being a man. Is that where you got your beard?" "I stole it from your Grandpa." "Ew! You're not old enough to be grandpa are you? Are you 16?" "I am as old as the mountains. I am a troll that eats rocks."

"HAHAHAHAHHAHA. But trolls don't exist!" "They do too!"

Xavier pulls Arianne's hair.

"To be a Kung-Fu master, you should never pull your sister's hair. Just big trolls like me like that." "Can I pull *your* hair then?" "No!"

I drag them through the house after dinner time, one clinging to each foot. "ARRGGGHH." "Oh, we're not heavy, are we? HEEEHEEE."

As I leave Xavier clambers up my long body and hugs me with every bone and sinew he knows to exist, and the lizard of my heart sheds its skin, the cracked soil of my skeleton melts into his unknowing.

written by Alex

CELEBRATING ALEX

19 SEPTEMBER 2015

Never in my life have I experienced the shock and devastation brought by the news of Alex ending his life – I loved him so much. I would have wanted to have been there for him and to try to save him. My heart breaks for Beatriz, Terry, Marena, Andrew, and Olive, Marianna and Ricardo – others in his family and close friends who are suffering unimaginable pain.

I was close to Alex in these last 12 years of his life. He liked to visit Ben and me, spend time on the beach and hang out with our friends Ruth and Robert, for whom he was a big hit. Our grandchildren, Xavier and Arianne adored him, and he – them. He could be a lot of fun, and so playful.

He was such a gift in our lives – exuding trust, appreciation, joyfulness and laughter. It was wonderful to be with him. Only rarely were we with him when he was deeply troubled.

I often thought about what it must have been like for Beatriz, Terry, Marena, Andrew and Olive. They loved him and tried to bring to bear the very best to strengthen him, imbue him with a sense of his gifts, and strengthen those gifts for his good, and the good of those around him. That is why, despite his illness, he was not only a beautiful man but he was also able to create amazing poetry, and was always able to engage and raise the spirits of his listeners.

What were his gifts? Besides that delicious laughter, he had an appreciation of people, nature, and literature. He had a questioning, exploring mind - a wonderful intellect which was enlarged by his inquisitiveness.

I enjoyed so much being with him. I felt challenged, but at the same time valued, loved and respected. He wanted to know if I've experienced telepathy, believed in God, thought he was a prophet. Because these were questions seldom explored in my everyday life — I enjoyed mining my thoughts.

Conversations with him were personal, deep and lively. He was searching for answers to his life. He thought of himself as a prophet. I don't deny — his questions were enlightened, and there was also a healing quality to his gentleness, kindness, and careful listening.

And there is the wonderful gift of his poetry. Alex could see beyond the usual and humdrum to the divine and spiritual, using brilliant metaphor that would pierce the heart or send the imagination dazzling. His mind touched heaven, the angels, the stars, heroes, the devil, the tragedy of materialism, and the suffering and fear of psychosis. He knew street people for whom he had great empathy and vividly portrayed their lives

Alex was born with glory in him. His light will shine in all of us – his warmth, love of life, his acceptance of those around him, his forgiving nature, his laughter and joyfulness.

Despite his suffering he gave so much.

Margot

Sixteen years of Love

Freely given, gentle heart

I'll not let you go

BEACH CONTEMPLATION

Kayaker

Splashes near my feet.

A half-crescent of sparkling sea.

The webbed claw and feathered corpse of a sea bird

whose spirit is here in the sea-smells.

Dried sea-weed mounds

And lovely jeweled light shedding small waves

revealing myriad colours on brightened stones.

Sun warms my fleecy jacket –

But the breeze is cool.

The lap/splash sounds get louder.

The hollow woof of the curving water finds my attention.

I love this moment. I treasure its fleetingness.

I long to hold onto it.

This is all I want!

A crab carapace rolls against the bird's body.

Seaweed wraps both dead things.

Not a bad place for a burial!

I'm being splashed! I don't want to move

but the beach-space is being eaten by the incoming tide.

Stay here forever. Die here! Like the sea-bird and crab.

Roll me in seaweed!

Let the tide take me to the forever and ever.

My spirit would be so grateful!

My bones rolling with currents

My bones becoming sand – being swum over gracefully

by fish.

Finally my minerals becoming the sea splashing on

many shores, floating sea-birds, reflecting sunlight,

being wind-blown

into giant, roaring and crashing waves —

thundering in praise of the beauty of the Earth.

Margot   July 2016

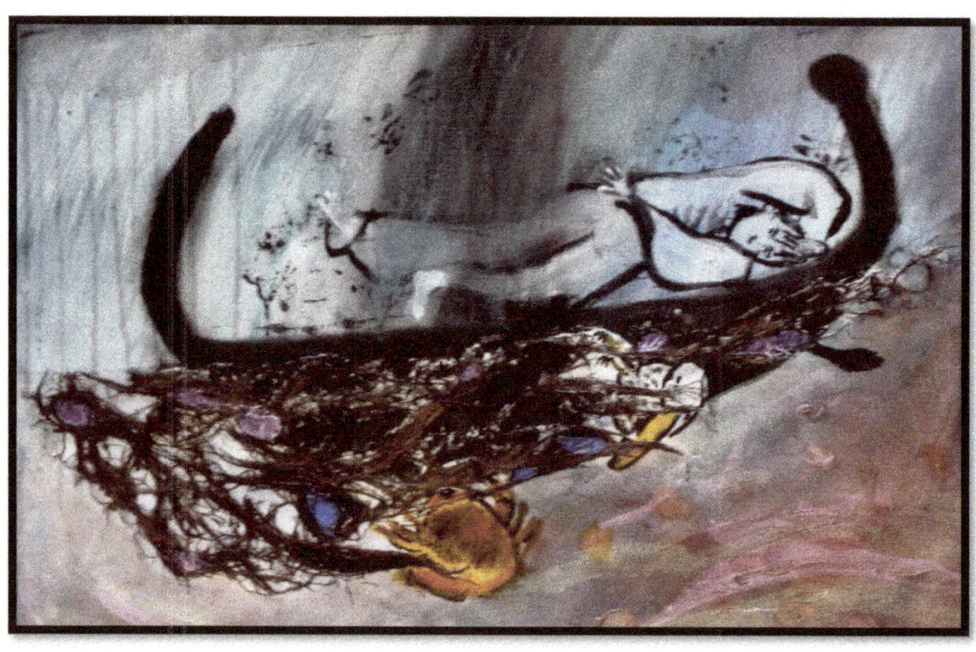

12 Beach Contemplation

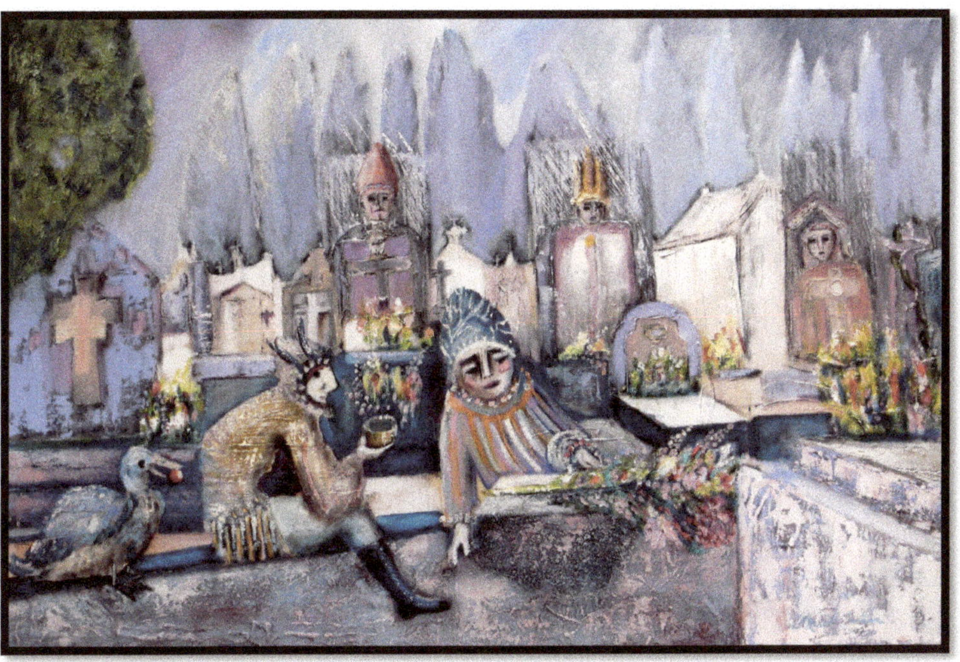

13   *Presences (Roussignon Graveyard)*

2006 – 30" x 48" – oil on canvas

dashing for the exit

You, dashing for the exit

I wanting to stay and taste still more.

Of course, we'd had our share.

Longer than many

Reminding us of so much done

So much yet to do.

Thoughts on a treadmill

New Beginnings

Seaweed floats in to nourish new life ashore.

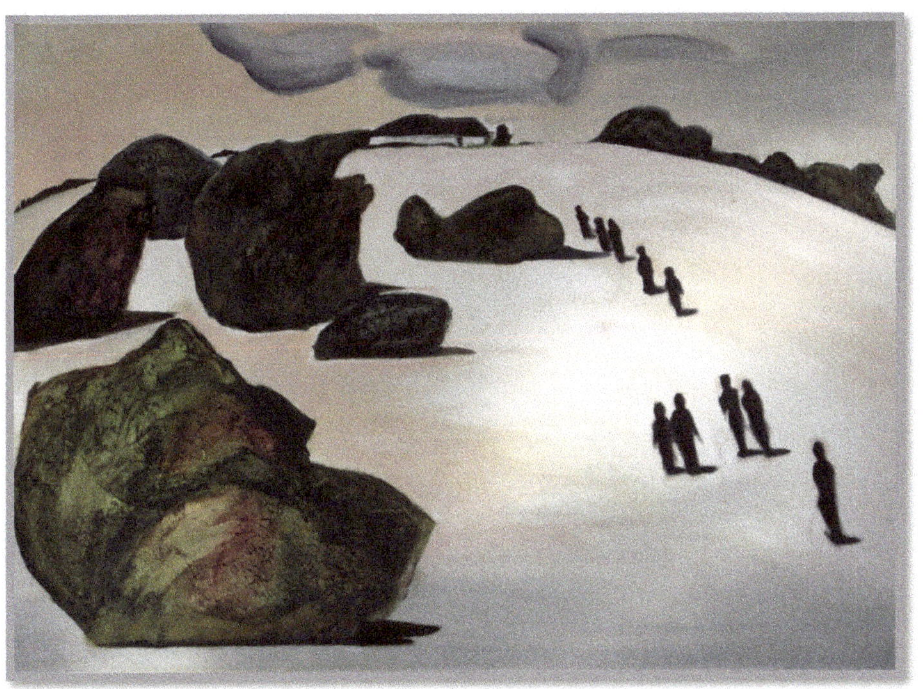

14   Beacon Hill
2000 – 3' x 4' – oil on canvas

Photographs

My Darling,

I look at photographs of you

and of the two of us together

at home in Crescent Beach,

with friends

or enjoying sunny travels
England,

> *Italy,*

>> *France,*

>>> *Mexico,*

>>>> *Germany,*

>>>>> *South America.*

You bless me with beautiful memories.

We're together

on a little green bus

in Ireland

sailing over ancient ruins

on a Turkish gullet.

A lifetime of adventures

tucked into our sixteen years together.

As long as I have and share

these memories of you,

I will never be totally alone.

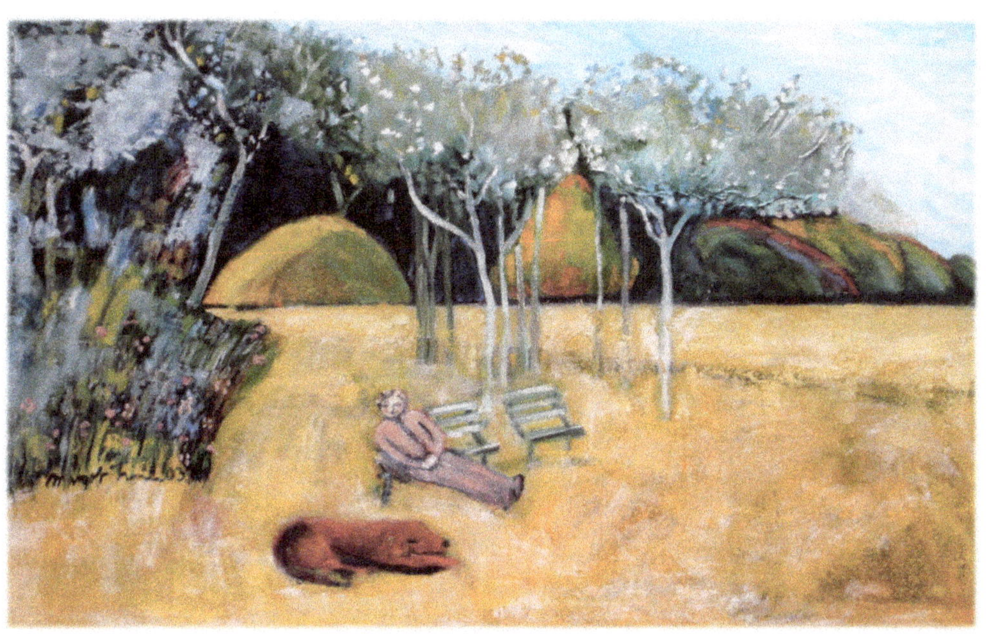

15 *Tranquility*
2002 – 2' x 3' – oil & encaustic on canvas

Tears

It's hard to talk about you with people.

Every now and then I bubble up

tears that can't be held back

flow.

Thank you for the beautiful years we spent together.

The best years of my life.

I Miss You by my Side

Sun seekers frolic in gentle waves

ice tinkles in my glass.

tourist-laden catamarans glide by

I Miss You by my Side.

Lovers stroll – honeymoon couples

children pluck crayfish from the reefs

delight at minnows nibbling their toes

I Miss You by my Side.

I sense your spirit on the sparkling sea

while Yellow-winged Caciques glide on thermal lift

and tiny sailboats skim the waves

I Miss You by my Side.

You're gone until we meet again

for now and in the years to come

I'll hold you in my heart

but Miss You by my Side.

Pablo Neruda:

When I die I want your hands on my eyes

When I die I want your hands on my eyes:

I want the light and the wheat of your beloved hands

to pass their freshness over me one more time

to feel the smoothness that changed my destiny.

I want you to live while I wait for you, asleep,

I want for your ears to go on hearing the wind,

for you to smell the sea that we loved together

and for you to go on walking the sand where we walked.

I want for what I love to go on living

and as for you I loved you and sang you above everything,

for that, go on flowering, flowery one,

so that you reach all that my love orders for you,

so that my shadow passes through your hair,

so that they know by this the reason for my song.

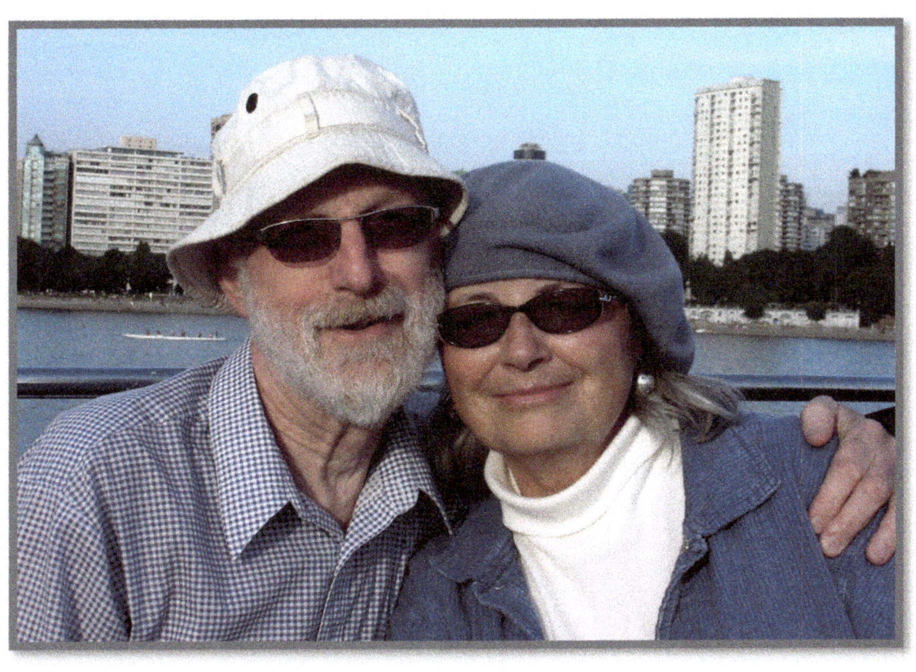

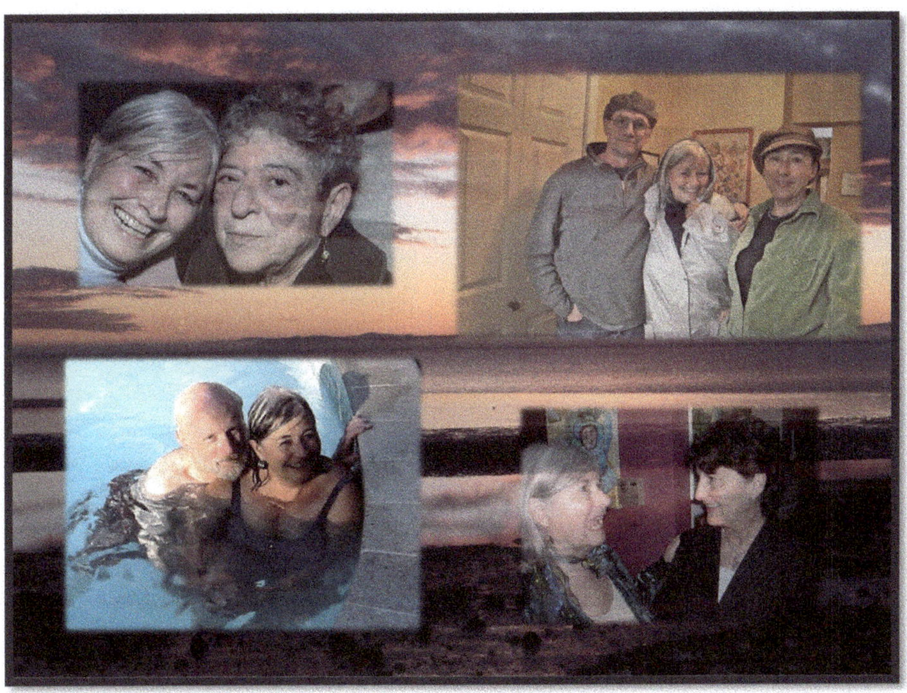

Going Home

Going home, going home

I am going home

Quiet like, some still day

I am going home

It's not far, just close by

Through an open door

Work all done, care laid by

Never fear no more

Mother's there expecting me

Father's waiting too

Lots of folks gathered there

All the friends I knew

I'm just going home

Going Home was based on Antonin Dvorak's "Largo" from his Symphony No. 9 (From the New World), Op. 95 *

Alone in May

Light two candles for company

cup of tea instead of wine

explore the green through dusty window panes

remembering how two loves rejoiced

in myriad tiny birds

no longer singing from the flowering vine

as if they know she's gone.

Stare down the telephone

it will not ring

no matter how you will it so

without her here to answer in her cheery tone.

When she was here the calls were every day

with happy chatter filled and ears in tune

to hear the briefest tale or sorrow told.

*   *   *   *

Last time I was alone

for ten long years

I had a tabby cat to sit

high on my chest

and purr the loneliness away.

I healed myself with pen and pad

upon that rocky hill.

My move and newfound love

gave truth to what I'd penned

and I believed once more

in innocence, forgiveness

and all that's whole and good.

You held my hand

taught me to walk again.

So now I write my tears

Listening to voices in my head.

We sat in company full sixteen years

until you had to leave.

I wait to join you in that other place

beyond all time

when I at last am called.

Ben   20 May, 2019

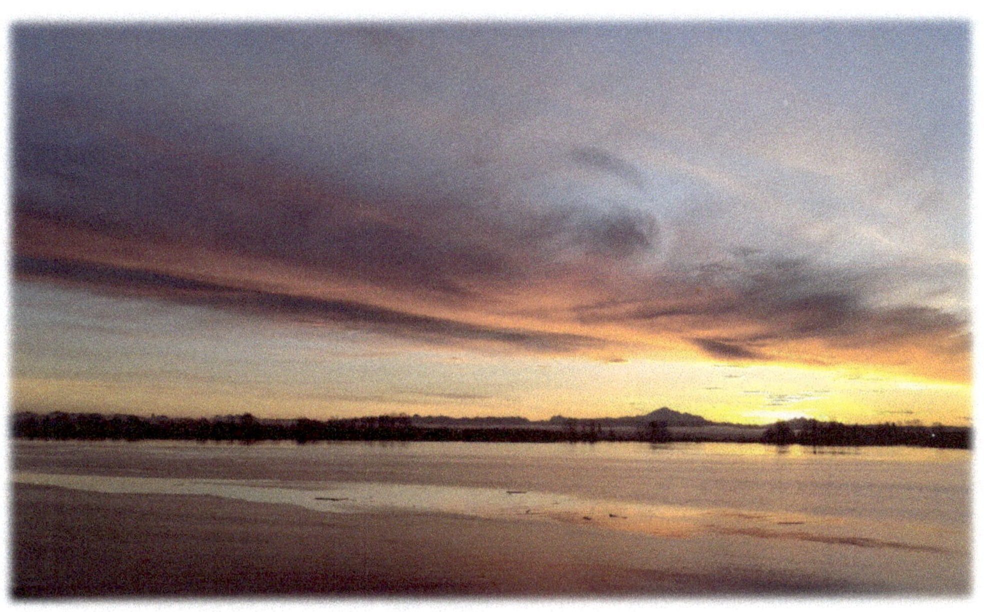

92

Margot's Paintings

* "Goin' Home" (p. 89) was actually written by one of Dvorak's pupils, William Arms Fisher (1861-1948), who adapted and arranged the Largo theme and added his own words, as indicated on the sheet music cover published by Oliver Ditson Company in Boston

Books by
Ben Nuttall-Smith

Mad God of the Toltecs, 2nd edition

Discovered in a Scream, 2nd edition

Henry Hamster Esquire

Crescent Beach Reflections

Flying With White Eagle

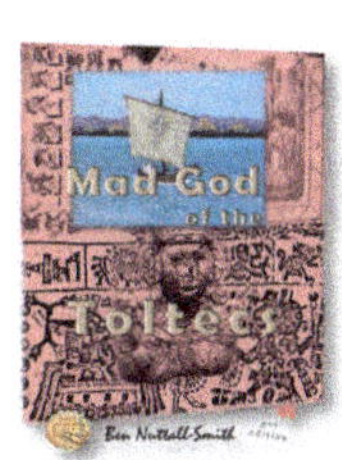
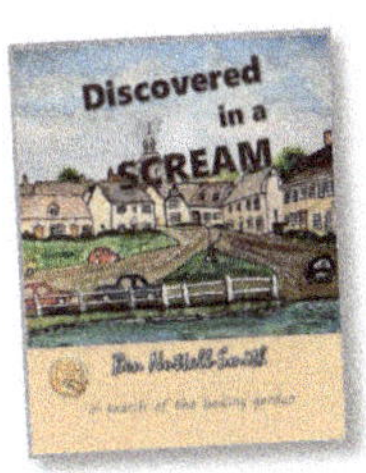
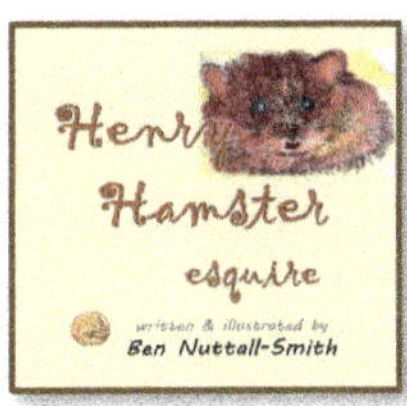
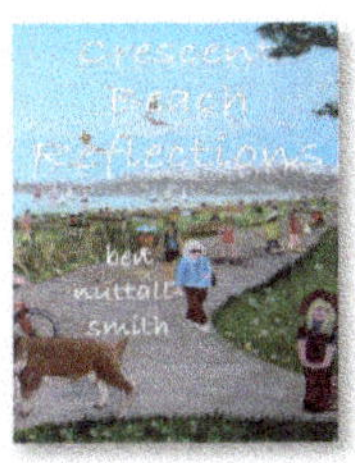
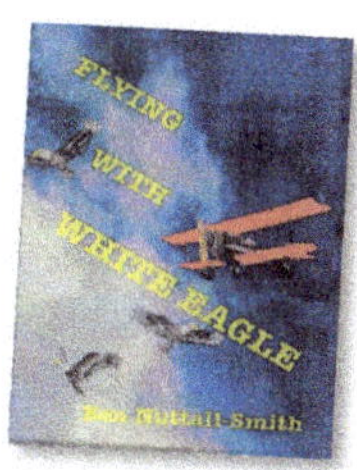

Available at **https://rutherfordpress.ca/**